ACT
American College Testing

by
Jerry Bobrow, Ph.D.

Contributing authors
Allan Casson, Ph.D.
Jean Eggenschwiler, M.A.
Rajiv Rimal, Ph.D.
Jeff Berkeley, M.S.
Karen Saenz, Ph.D.

Consultant
Don Gallaher, M.S.

Wiley Publishing, Inc.

Acknowledgments

I would like to thank Michele Spence of Cliffs Notes for her many, many, many hours of editing and making sure that I was on schedule. Meeting the deadlines would have been impossible without her careful review and extra efforts. I would also like to thank Stan Spence of Dragon Lake Graphics for his outstanding work on the final figures and diagrams. Finally, I would like to thank my wife, Susan, daughter, Jennifer (21), and sons, Adam (18) and Jonathan (14) for their patience, moral support, and comic relief.

Cover Photograph

Jean F. Podevin/The Image Bank

CliffsQuickReview™ *ACT*
Published by
Wiley Publishing, Inc.
909 Third Avenue
New York, NY 10022
www.wiley.com

Your ACT score can make the difference!
in the college or university you attend.

Cliffs Quick Review ACT **can make the difference!**
in the score you get.

So don't take a chance—take an advantage. *Cliffs Quick Review ACT* was written by leading experts in the field of test preparation, experts who have administered graduate, college entrance, and teacher credentialing test preparation programs for most of the California State Universities for over twenty years. Get the advantage of their expertise and the insights they give you by following this six-step approach:

- **Be aware.** Know as much as you possibly can about the exam before you walk in. This Cliffs Quick Review gives you this important information in a clear and easy-to-understand way.

- **Set a goal.** Call some of the schools you're interested in and see what score you need to be accepted there. This Cliffs Quick Review includes easy-to-use charts to help you set your goal.

- **Know the basic skills.** This Cliffs Quick Review will help you focus on which skills to review and will help you review those skills with practice questions and easy-to-follow, complete explanations.

- **Understand the question types.** This Cliffs Quick Review carefully analyzes each type of question so that you'll understand how to focus on what is being asked.

- **Learn strategies.** This Cliffs Quick Review emphasizes strategies and techniques for answering each type of question and includes samples that show you what to look for and how to apply each strategy.

- **Practice.** This Cliffs Quick Review includes a practice exam with answers, complete explanations, and analysis charts to help you spot your strengths and weaknesses.

Because your study time is valuable, you need this clear, effective, and easy-to-use guide to give you maximum benefit in a reasonable time. Using *Cliffs Quick Review ACT* and studying regularly will give you the edge in doing your best!

INTRODUCTION

PRACTICE TEST

SCORING AND COMPLETE ANSWERS AND EXPLANATIONS FOR THE PRACTICE TEST

INTRODUCTION

$\mathbf{T}$he ACT Assessment Program is a two-phase program that helps you make important decisions about your future.

- In the first phase, the ACT Interest Inventory and the ACT Student Profile sections collect information about your past experiences, your interests, and your goals. You'll complete these sections when you register for the ACT Assessment.

- The second phase, the ACT Assessment, is a battery of tests you'll take that cover four subject areas: English, mathematics, reading, and science reasoning.

Following are a circle graph and two charts showing the format commonly seen on the ACT Assessment and the test score ranges.

Exam sections and time allotments

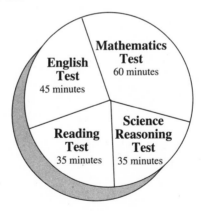

Commonly seen arrangement of sections, time allotments, and number of questions

COMMON FORMAT OF THE ACT		
Test 1 45 minutes	**English Test**	**75 Questions**
Test 2 60 minutes	**Mathematics Test**	**60 Questions**
Test 3 35 minutes	**Reading Test**	**40 Questions**
Test 4 35 minutes	**Science Reasoning Test**	**40 Questions**
Total Testing Time 175 minutes = 2 hours, 55 minutes Approximately 215 questions		

Test scores

The four tests generate four individual test scores, a composite score (which is the average of the four test scores), and seven subscores.

ACT SCORE RANGES
English Test   1 – 36
Subscores:
usage/mechanics   1 – 18
rhetorical skills   1 – 18
Mathematics Test   1 – 36
Subscores:
pre-algebra/elementary algebra   1 – 18
intermediate algebra/coordinate geometry   1 – 18
plane geometry/trigonometry   1 – 18
Reading Test   1 – 36
Subscores:
social studies/sciences   1 – 18
arts/literature   1 – 18
Science Reasoning Test   1 – 36
Composite Score   1 – 36

What is the New ACT Writing Test?

The ACT Writing Test is a 30-minute test, which is optional, that measures your skill in planning and writing a short essay.

Do I have to take the Writing Test?

Some colleges will require the Writing Test; others will not. Most colleges will accept scores from the Writing Test even if they do not require it. You should check directly with the schools to which you are applying to see if the Writing Test is required.

Can I take the Writing Test by itself? That is, can I take the Writing Test without taking the multiple-choice test?

No.

How is the Writing Test scored?

The essays are graded by two experienced professional readers on a six-point scale (total possible is 2 to 12). The scores reported to you and to the colleges you designate will include a scaled score, from 1 to 36, that reflects the performance on the Writing Test and the English Test combined. A second Writing Test subscore on a 2 to 12 scale reflects your writing score.

What kind of topics will be given for the Writing Test?

The essay topics are ones that all high school students should be able to write about, and that allow them to take one side or the other or to present their own perspective.

Who administers the ACT?

The ACT is administered by the American College Testing Program. For further information about the ACT Assessment Program, write to ACTP, P.O. Box 168, Iowa City, IA, 52243-0168, call 319-337-1000, or check the ACT World Wide Web site at http://www.act.org.

What is the structure of the ACT Assessment?

The ACT Assessment consists of four tests. The English Test contains 75 questions and lasts 45 minutes. The Mathematics Test contains 60 questions and lasts 60 minutes. The Reading Test contains 40 questions and lasts 35 minutes. The Science Reasoning Test contains 40 questions and lasts 35 minutes. All four tests consist exclusively of multiple-choice questions.

How is the ACT Assessment scored?

Each of the tests is scored from 1 to 36, with a mean score of 18. The subscores within sections are scored from 1 to 18, with a mean score of 9. The composite score is from 1 to 36.

How do colleges use the information on my SPR?

Most colleges use the information on your Student Profile Report in two ways: (1) as part of the admission process, to assess your ability to do college-level work, and (2) to help you plan your program of study.

May I take the ACT Assessment more than once?

Yes, you may, but you should try to take it only once and do your best. If you do need to take the test a second time, check the registration/information bulletin for registration procedures.

What materials may I bring to the ACT?

You *should* bring

—your test center admission ticket
—acceptable identification (your admission ticket is *not* identification)
—several sharpened number 2 pencils
—a good eraser
—a watch (alarms must be turned off on watches)
—an acceptable calculator (for the mathematics section of the assessment only)

See the registration booklet for a description of required identification and acceptable calculators. *No* books, notes, highlighters, or scratch paper are permitted. Room for your figuring will be provided in the test booklet itself. Phones, pagers, food or drink, or other reading materials are also *not* permitted.

May I cancel my score?

Yes. You may do so by notifying your test supervisor before you leave the examination, or you may cancel your test scores by calling 319-337-1270 no *later* than 12 noon, Central time, on the *Thursday* immediately following your test date.

Should I guess on the test?

Yes, guess if you don't know the answer. There's no penalty for guessing, so it's to your advantage to answer every question.

How should I prepare for the ACT Assessment?

Understanding and practicing test-taking strategies will help a great deal. Subject matter review is particularly useful for the Mathematics Test and the English Test.

How and when should I register?

The registration period opens about ten weeks before the test date and closes about four weeks before the test date. To register within this period, obtain an ACT registration/information booklet from your high school counselor and follow the registration instructions it includes.

If you're registering for the first time, you can register in two ways: (1) by paper folder included in the registration bulletin or (2) by using ACT's home page on the World Wide Web (http://www.act.org). For this method of registration, payment must be made by VISA or MasterCard.

If you're reregistering, that is, if you're in high school and have taken the ACT within the last two years on a national test date, you don't have to complete the entire folder, since your record should already be on file. There are three ways you can *re*register: (1) by telephone (the toll-free number is 1-800-525-6926; payment must be made by VISA or MasterCard, and there is a $10 additional fee for phone *re*registration), (2) by using ACT's home page on the World Wide Web (http://www.act.org; payment must be made by VISA or MasterCard), or (3) by paper folder included in the registration bulletin (pay special attention to *re*registration tips given throughout the bulletin.

Regardless of how you register, pay special attention to the registration deadlines.

What if I miss the registration deadlines?

You're encouraged to register *before* the deadlines, but there is a late registration period. If you register during the late registration period, there is an additional fee. If you miss the late registration deadline, you could try to take the test as a "standby." To do so, you must arrive early (before 8:00 a.m.) and realize that you will be admitted after the registered students have been admitted, but only if space and materials are available. *There is no guarantee that you'll be admitted as a "standby."* "Standby" test takers should check the information bulletin for materials to bring, method of payment, and additional fee required.

What if I can't take the regular Saturday administration because of religious beliefs?

Most states have non-Saturday test centers. Check your registration bulletin for a listing of states and the dates on which non-Saturday testing is given. For additional information, call ACT at 319-337-1270 or write to ACT Registration, P.O. Box 414, Iowa City, IA 52243-0414. (If a non-Saturday testing center is more than 50 miles from your home, call 319-337-1332 or write to ACT Universal Testing, P.O. Box 4028, Iowa City, IA 52243-4028.)

What if I have a diagnosed disability or am confined to a hospital? Can special arrangements be made?

ACT attempts to make special arrangements whenever possible. For more information, call 319-337-1332 or write to ACT Universal Testing, P.O. Box 4028, Iowa City, IA 52243-4028.

How often is the test given?

The test is given five or six times year, depending on your location. The test is usually given in October, December, February, April, and June. At some locations, it's also given in September. Regular administrations are on Saturday morning.

Key Strategies for a Positive Approach to the Exam

The key to doing well on the ACT Assessment is to use these positive, active strategies both in your preparation and when you take the exam.

- Set a goal.
- Review basic skills necessary.
- Know the directions.
- Look for winners.
- Don't get stuck.
- Eliminate.
- If you don't know the answer, guess.
- Don't misread.
- Use a multiple-multiple-choice technique.
- Practice, practice, practice.
- Erase extra marks on your answer sheet.

Set a goal. Contact the colleges or universities you're interested in attending and find out the scores you'll need to get in. (The *Official College Handbook,* published by the College Board, can also give you this valuable information.) Once you've reviewed the scores necessary or the average scores for the schools, then set your personal goals. The following charts, showing the *approximate* number of questions you need to get right to achieve a particular score, will help you do that. In these charts, **check the scores you wish to work toward.**

English Test

	Score	Approximate % right
	36	100
	33	97 – 98
	30	92 – 93
	27	83 – 85
	24	73 – 75
	21	64 – 65
	18	53 – 55
	15	42 – 44
	12	31 – 35

Mathematics Test

	Score	Approximate % right
	36	100
	33	97 – 98
	30	89 – 90
	27	77 – 79
	24	67 – 69
	21	57 – 59
	18	45 – 46
	15	28 – 29
	12	17 – 19

Reading Test

	Score	Approximate % right
	36	99 – 100
	33	90 – 93
	30	81 – 88
	27	74 – 80
	24	64 – 70
	21	55 – 60
	18	45 – 48
	15	38 – 42
	12	30 – 33

Science Reasoning Test

Score	Approximate % right
36	100
33	95 – 98
30	89 – 93
27	81 – 85
24	71 – 75
21	53 – 58
18	45 – 48
15	33 – 34
12	24 – 30

your English score goal _____
+ your math score goal _____
+ your reading score goal _____
+ your science reasoning score goal _____
= your total score goal _____ **divided by 4**

= your composite score goal _____

Review basic skills necessary. As you begin your preparation, you should review the basic skills you need to do well. For the English Test, a review of grammar, punctuation, sentence structure, style, and organization of writing will be helpful. For the Mathematics Test, a review of arithmetic, pre-algebra, elementary and intermediate algebra, coordinate and plane geometry, and trigonometry will give you a good foundation. For the Reading Test, working on reading comprehension skills will be helpful. A short method to help improve some reading skills is to quickly read an article from a magazine and then summarize the main point of the article in one sentence. To make this method most effective, write out each sentence and repeat the exercise with at least four or five articles. For the Science Reasoning Test, reviewing some basic scientific terms and facts in biology, earth/space science, chemistry, and physics, along with reviewing simple arithmetic computations, will give you a good basis. While you don't need advanced knowledge in these sciences, you may need some basic background knowledge.

Know the directions. Read and review the directions for each of the four tests carefully before the day of the exam so that you'll be completely familiar with them.

Look for winners. Go into each test section looking for questions you can answer and should get right. Keep in mind that the questions in each test are not in order of difficulty (except for the Mathematics Test, which is slightly graduated in difficulty), so a difficult question could be followed by an easy one. Remember, *the basis for a good score is getting the questions right that you can and should get right.*

Don't get stuck. Since each question within one of the four tests is worth the same amount, you should never get stuck on any one question. Using the following marking system in your question booklet can help.

1. Answer easy questions immediately.

2. When you come to a question that seems "impossible" to answer, mark a large – (minus sign) next to it on your test booklet.

3. Then mark a "guess" answer on your answer sheet and move on to the next question.

4. When you come to a question that seems solvable but appears too time consuming, mark a large + (plus sign) next to that question in your test booklet and register a guess answer on your answer sheet. Then move on to the next question.

Since your time allotment is usually less than a minute per question, a "time-consuming" question is a question that you estimate will take you more than a minute or a minute and a half to answer. But don't waste time deciding whether a question is a plus or a minus. Act quickly, as the intent of this strategy is, in fact, to save you valuable time. After you work all your easy questions, your booklet should look something like this.

$$
\begin{aligned}
&1.\\
&+2.\\
&3.\\
&-4.\\
&+5.\\
&\quad\text{etc.}
\end{aligned}
$$

5. After answering all the questions you can immediately answer, go back and work on your + questions. Change your "guess" on your answer sheet, if necessary, for those questions you're able to answer.

6. If you finish answering your + questions and still have time left, you can either

   —try your – questions, those you considered impossible. Sometimes a question later in the section will "trigger" your memory and you'll be able to go back and answer one of those earlier questions.

   —or simply not bother with those impossible questions. Rather, you can spend your time reviewing your work to be sure you didn't make any careless mistakes on the questions you thought were easy to answer.

Remember, you don't have to erase the pluses and minuses you made on your *question booklet.* And be sure to fill in all your answer spaces—if necessary, with a guess. As there is no penalty for wrong answers, it makes no sense to leave an answer space blank. And, of course, remember that you may work only in one section of the test at a time.

Knowing when to skip a question is invaluable, so keep in mind that you should never get stuck on any one question. As mentioned earlier, you should *never* spend more than a minute or a minute and a half on any one question.

Eliminate. As soon as you know that an answer choice is wrong, eliminate it. As you eliminate an answer choice from consideration, take advantage of being allowed to mark in your testing booklet by marking out the eliminated answer in your question booklet as follows:

$$? \text{ A.}$$
$$\cancel{B}.$$
$$\cancel{C}.$$
$$? \text{ D.}$$

Notice that some choices are marked with question marks, signifying that they may be possible answers. This technique will help you avoid reconsidering those choices you've already eliminated and will help you narrow down your possible answers. Again, remember that these marks in your testing booklet do not need to be erased.

If you don't know the answer, guess. Since there's no penalty for guessing on the ACT, *you should never leave a question without at least taking a guess.* Keep in mind that you can often eliminate ridiculous or unreasonable answers—making your guess an educated guess. If you're about to run out of time, fill in a guess answer on the remaining questions. Don't leave any unanswered questions.

Don't misread. One of the most common mistakes on most exams is misreading the question. You must be sure you know what the question is asking. For example,

1. If $5x + 7 = 32$, what is the value of $x + 2$?

   Notice that this question doesn't ask for the value of x, but rather the value of $x + 2$.

Or

2. All of the following statements could be true EXCEPT . . .

Or

3. Which of the following is NOT a possible explanation . . .?

   Notice that the words EXCEPT and NOT change these questions significantly.

To avoid misreading a question (and therefore answering it incorrectly), simply *underline or circle* what you must answer in the question. For example, do you have to find x or $x + 2$? Are you looking for what could be true or the *exception* to what could be true? To help in avoiding misreads, mark the questions in your booklet in this way.

1. If $5x + 7 = 32$, what is the value of <u>$x + 2$</u>?

2. All of the following statements <u>could</u> be true <u>EXCEPT</u> . . .

3. Which of the following is <u>NOT</u> a <u>possible explanation</u> . . .?

Once again, these underlines or circles in your question booklet do not have to be erased.

Use a multiple-multiple-choice technique. Some math and verbal questions use a "multiple-multiple-choice" format. At first glance, these questions appear more confusing and more difficult than normal four- or five-choice (**A, B, C, D, E**) multiple-choice questions. Actually, once you understand "multiple-multiple-choice" question types and the techniques you can use to answer them, they are often easier than comparable multiple-choice questions. For example,

4. If x is a positive integer, then which of the following must be true?

    I. $x > 0$
   II. $x = 0$
  III. $x < 1$

   F. I only
   G. II only
   H. III only
   J. I and II only
   K. I and III only

Since x is a positive integer, it must be a counting number. Note that possible values of x could be 1, or 2, or 3, or 4, and so on. Therefore, statement I, $x > 0$, is always true. So next to I on your question booklet, place a T for *true*.

      T I. $x > 0$
          II. $x = 0$
        III. $x < 1$

Now realize that the correct final answer choice (**F, G, H, J,** or **K**) *must* contain *true statement I*. This eliminates **G** and **H** as possible correct answer choices, as they do *not* contain true statement I. You should cross out **G** and **H** on your question booklet.

Statement II is *incorrect.* If x is positive, x can't equal zero. So next to II, you should place an F for *false*.

T I. $x > 0$
F II. $x = 0$
    III. $x < 1$

Knowing that II is false allows you to eliminate any answer choices that contain *false statement II*. Therefore, you should cross out **J,** as it contains false statement II. Only **F** and **K** are left as possible correct answers.

Finally, you realize that statement III is also false, as x must be 1 or greater. So you place an F next to III, thus eliminating choice **K** and leaving **F,** I only. This technique often saves some precious time and allows you to take a better educated guess should you not be able to complete all parts (I, II, and III) of a multiple-multiple-choice question.

Practice, practice, practice. Nothing beats practice. You can't practice too much. But the important thing in practicing is to learn from your mistakes, so it's important that you go back and carefully analyze and correct your mistakes. Analyzing and correcting will help you focus your review and eliminate your common mistakes. When you practice, try to simulate the testing conditions—that is, no scratch paper, a small desk, no books, including dictionaries, and so forth. The only difference between your practice and the real thing is that when you practice, you should short yourself slightly on time. Instead of giving yourself 45 minutes on the English Test, for example, give yourself 40 or 41 minutes, which will help you work at a good pace.

Erase extra marks on your answer sheet. Because the scoring machine may count extra marks on the answer sheet as wrong answers, be sure to erase any you've put there before time is up.

THE BASICS, THE QUESTIONS, AND THE KEY STRATEGIES FOR THE ACT TEST SECTIONS

The Skills You'll Use

The English Test asseses your ablility to

- recognize and correct errors in standard written English
- use your knowledge of grammar, punctuation, sentence structure, and rhetoric

Your English Test Score

You have a total of 45 minutes to complete 75 items. The total English Test is scored from 1 to 36, with a mean score of 18. In addition to the total English Test score, two subscores are reported in the following areas.

- usage/mechanics (40 items)
- rhetorical skills (35 items)

The subscores range from 1 to 18, with a mean score of 9.

The Directions

In the left-hand column, you will find passages in a "spread-out" format with various words and phrases underlined and numbered. In the right-hand column, you will find a set of responses corresponding to each underlined portion. If the underlined portion is correct standard written English, is most appropriate to the style and feeling of the passage, or best makes the intended statement, mark the letter indicating "NO CHANGE." If the underlined portion is not the best choice given, choose the one that is. For these questions, consider only the underlined portions; assume that the rest of the passage is correct as written. You will also see questions concerning parts of the passage or the whole passage. Choose the response you feel is best for these questions.

For some passages, you may also be given a box of additional directions similar to the following.

> The following paragraphs are given a number in brackets above each one. The paragraphs may be in the most logical order, or they may not. Item ___ asks you to choose the paragraph sequence that is the most logical.

The Types of English Test Questions

The English Test consists of two types of questions.

- usage and mechanics
- rhetorical skills

The following graph and table show the general breakdown of the English questions by category.

**Types of
English Questions**

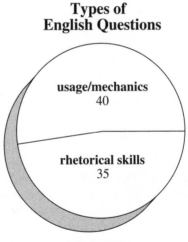

75 Total Items

ENGLISH CONTENT AREA BREAKDOWN
(approximate percentages)

Content	Number of Items	Percentages
Usage/Mechanics	40	53%
punctuation	10	13%
grammar and usage	12	16%
sentence structure	18	24%
Rhetorical skills	35	47%
strategy	12	16%
organization	11	15%
style	12	16%
Total	75	

General Strategies for Any English Test Question

- Pace yourself. Remember, you have about 30 seconds to answer each question, so establish a good pace.

- Understand the context. Reading the sentence before and after the sentence in question can help put your answer in context. Sometimes you may wish to skim the paragraph before answering the questions. Skimming can be particularly beneficial on questions involving sentence order.

- Reread with your answer. Once you've selected an answer, try to quickly reread the sentence with your answer to make sure it fits.

- Note the style and tone of the passage. The style and tone of the passage will often help you eliminate answer choices that "just don't sound right."

- Eliminate answers with mistakes. You may be able to eliminate some choices because they contain grammar or usage errors.

- Be aware of making new mistakes. Sometimes as you select a choice that looks good, you may find that you've created another mistake. Reading the sentence with your answer will help here too.

- Watch for differences in choices. Sometimes more than one choice may seem correct, but a closer look at the differences can lead you to the best choice.

- Notice questions about a section or the entire passage. A number with a box around it (such as ⑫) tips you off that the question is about a section. Boxed instructions such as the following also identify these types of questions.

> Question 34 asks about the passage as a whole.

The Types of Usage and Mechanics Questions

The usage and mechanics questions may be based on any of these categories.

- punctuation, with an emphasis on punctuation that influences meaning, such as that which avoids ambiguity or identifies an appositive

- grammar and usage, such as agreement, case, verb form, and idiomatic usage

- sentence structure, including correct subordination, parallelism, and placement of modifiers

The following graph shows the general breakdown of the usage and mechanics questions by category.

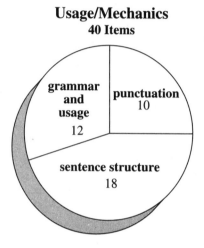

Usage/Mechanics
40 Items

grammar and usage
12

punctuation
10

sentence structure
18

Samples and Key Strategies for the Usage and Mechanics Questions

- Know the common punctuation errors.

- Understand the basics of standard grammar and usage.

- Note the sentence structure, the relationship of parts of the sentence.

Know the common punctuation errors. These questions test your knowledge of correct punctuation both at the end of and within sentences. You should be familiar with the use of the period, question mark, exclamation point, comma, semicolon, colon, dash, apostrophe, parentheses, and quotation marks.

Samples:

In Maryland, toxic chemicals in the water have led to widespread deformities in <u>frogs; missing limbs</u>
                                          1   2

1. **A.** NO CHANGE
   B. frogs:
   C. frogs.
   D. frogs

<u>extra limbs, and missing organs.</u>
                    2
Scientists are now trying to identify the chemicals in the water that

2. **F.** NO CHANGE
   G. limbs, extra limbs, and missing organs.
   H. and extra limbs, and missing organs.
   J. limbs extra limbs and missing organs.

cause the <u>deformities, they hope</u> to
                              3
isolate them before any humans have been harmed.

3. **A.** NO CHANGE
   B. deformities: they hope
   C. deformities; they hope
   D. deformities, they are hoping

Answers:

1. **B** The colon is used to introduce a list. Using either a semi-colon, choice **A,** or a period, choice **B,** would create a sentence fragment, since the words that follow the punctuation are not a complete sentence as there is no verb. Choice **D** is incorrect because some punctuation is necessary here; you could use a comma instead of the colon, but that choice isn't given.

2. **G** This series requires two commas, one after each use of the word *limbs.* Choice **H** is incorrect because the revision reduces the series of three to only two parts, so a comma isn't necessary.

3. **C** The correct punctuation is the semicolon, which is used, like a period, to separate two independent clauses. You should use a colon to introduce a list or a restatement. Choice **D** is a comma splice; using only a comma to separate two independent clauses creates a run-on sentence.

Understand the basics of standard grammar and usage. These questions test your knowledge of basic grammar and usage, including subject-verb and pronoun-antecedent agreement (agreement between the pronoun and the word it refers to). They also test the case of pronouns, verb forms, and idiomatic usage.

Samples:

Frank Lloyd Wright is the one architect <u>who most Americans have heard of.</u> His picture
4

4. F. NO CHANGE
   G. who most Americans know about.
   H. whom most Americans have heard of.
   J. which most Americans have heard about.

<u>has appeared</u> on a postage stamp, and many books and television programs have celebrated his designs. Though his achievements
5

5. A. NO CHANGE
   B. having appeared
   C. appearing
   D. appeared

<u>is revered</u> around the world, his legacy is often neglected in the United States, where several houses have been destroyed by fire.
6

6. F. NO CHANGE
   G. has been revered
   H. are revered
   J. were revered

Answers:

4. H Since the pronoun here is the object of the preposition *of,* the objective case *(whom)* is needed.

5. A The original sentence is correct. The verb should be singular to agree with *picture,* and the present perfect tense *(has appeared)* is consistent with *have celebrated* later in the sentence.

6. H There is an agreement error here, with a singular verb and a plural subject *(achievements)*. The correct form is *are revered.* This present perfect verb tense is consistent with *is neglected.*

Note the sentence structure, the relationship of parts of the sentence. These questions test your knowledge of the relationship of the parts of the sentence: coordination and subordination, parallel construction, and correct placement of modifiers.

Samples:

Mine is a family of pro-
crastinators. Influenced by the
habits of my older brothers and
sisters, <u>my homework is always
the last thing I do.</u> Whether it is
washing the car, mowing the lawn,

7. A. NO CHANGE
   B. the last thing I do is
      my homework.
   C. at the last minute is
      when I do my
      homework.
   D. I do my homework at
      the last minute.

<u>or if I have to clean out the garage,</u>
I always put a job off as long as I
can. And my grandfather does

8. F. NO CHANGE
   G. or cleaning out the
      garage,
   H. or if the garage needs
      cleaning,
   J. or the garage being
      cleaned out,

<u>even at his age,</u> the same thing.

9. A. NO CHANGE
   B. (Add a comma before
      the underlined phrase
      and place it after
      grandfather.)
   C. (Place the underlined
      phrase after *same.*)
   D. OMIT the underlined
      portion.

Answers:

7. **D** In all three other versions of the sentence, the participial phrase at the beginning, *Influenced by the habits of my older brothers and sisters,* dangles. That is, the word it modifies (the *I,* not the *homework,* has been *influenced*) is not positioned next to the phrase. Only choice **D** corrects this error.

8. **G** The error of construction here is faulty parallelism. The series begins with *washing* and *mowing* (two verbal nouns), but the third part has a different form in choices **F, H,** and **J.** Choice **G** correctly uses a parallel third term, *cleaning.*

9. **B** The phrase *even at his age* should be placed as close to the noun it refers to (*grandfather*) as possible, and the phrase should be set off by commas. Omitting the underlined portion changes the meaning.

The Types of Rhetorical Skills Questions

The rhetorical skills questions may be based on any of these categories.

- strategy, including questions about the audience, purpose, and effectiveness of prose

- organization, including questions about the order, unity, and coherence of a passage

- style, including questions about diction, imagery, freedom from ambiguity, and economy in writing

The following graph shows the general breakdown of the rhetorical skills questions by category.

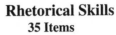

Rhetorical Skills
35 Items

Samples and Key Strategies for the
Rhetorical Skills Questions

- Pay special attention to the relationship of language to audience and to the author's strategy and purpose.

- Notice how well the paragraph or essay is organized.

- Watch for precise, appropriate use of language, the style of the passage.

Pay special attention to the relationship of language to audience and to the author's strategy and purpose. These questions test your understanding of the relationship of language to audience and purpose. They examine your ability to revise, to add or delete material, to handle transitions, and to open and close an essay effectively.

Samples:

Why are spiders not caught in their own webs? Some webs, like those of the trapdoor spider are not sticky, but are simply a device to alert the spider of the position of the prey. <u>The webs of spiders have many shapes.</u> In the sticky webs, the spiders leave paths that are not sticky that they can follow.
₁₀
₁₀

10. F. NO CHANGE
  G. Spider webs, how-ever, have many shapes.
  H. The webs of the spi-der may have many different shapes.
  J. OMIT the underlined portion.

<u>In addition,</u> the orb spider's web is sticky only on its circle, while the spokes are not. The prey is caught between the spokes.
₁₁

11. A. NO CHANGE
  B. However,
  C. For example,
  D. On the other hand,

Item 12 poses a question about the essay as a whole.

12. For which of the follow-ing audiences would this paragraph be most appropriate?
  F. Preschool children
  G. Young readers with an interest in science
  H. College seniors majoring in zoology
  J. Graduate students in entomology

Answers:

10. J The sentence should be deleted. It isn't relevant to the subject of the paragraph, why spiders are not caught in their own webs.

11. C The introductory phrase shouldn't mark a change of direction, as in choices **B** and **D**. The sentence supplies an example of a web with a safe path for the spider.

12. G The passage is too difficult for preschool children and probably too elementary for college or graduate school students.

Notice how well the paragraph or essay is organized. These questions test your understanding of how well a paragraph or the essay as a whole is organized. They examine order and coherence, the relevance of the parts to the whole.

Samples:

[1] Surprisingly, the number of small publishing companies in the United States has been slowly growing. [2] One successful company publishes only biography— about twelve each year. [3] Another publishes thirty or forty reprints annually. [4] The giants of the industry account for only forty-nine percent of the books sold each month at large chain stores like Barnes & Noble. ⑬ ⑭

13. The author is considering a change in the order of the four sentences in this paragraph. Which of the following is the most effective order?

   A. NO CHANGE
   B. 2, 3, 4, 1
   C. 2, 3, 1, 4
   D. 4, 1, 2, 3

14. The author wishes to add the following detail to this paragraph:

   "Just over half of the sales are books from small publishers or university presses."

   The most effective place for the new sentence is:

   F. after Sentence 1.
   G. after Sentence 2.
   H. after Sentence 3.
   J. after Sentence 4.

Answers:

13. **A** The paragraph is well organized as it now stands. The first sentence clearly states the central subject, the second and third add supporting details, and the fourth supplies additional evidence and a summing up.

14. **J** The sentence fits most logically at the end of the paragraph. It explains more fully who publishes the books that aren't supplied by the large publishing companies. Although the sentence might follow the first sentence, this position makes the transition to the sentence that follows awkward.

Watch for precise, appropriate use of language, the style of the passage. These questions test your mastery of diction and tone. They raise the issues of precise and appropriate use of language and the avoidance of ambiguity, clichés, and wordiness.

Samples:

In the 1947 film *A Double Life,* Ronald Coleman is a modern actor who is playing <u>the title role of Othello</u> in Shakespeare's *Othello.*
₁₅

15. **A.** NO CHANGE
    B. Othello, the title role,
    C. the role of Othello
    D. the title role

In the course of the film, <u>he loses it</u> as the murderous jealousy of the character in the play seeps into his
₁₆

16. **F.** NO CHANGE
    G. he goes off his rocker
    H. he goes mad
    J. he becomes insane and mad

real life. <u>In the final analysis,</u> the movie is an effective study of a disintegrating mind.
₁₇

17. **A.** NO CHANGE
    B. To all intents and purposes,
    C. When all is said and done,
    D. OMIT the underlined portion.

Answers:

15. D The original phrase is repetitive. The title role of the play *Othello* is Othello; there is no need to repeat the word. Saying only *the title role* avoids any redundancy.

16. H The errors here are in level of style. The slang of choices **F** and **G** is out of keeping with the word choice (diction) in the rest of the paragraph. Choice **J** is redundant, as *mad* and *insane* mean the same thing.

17. D The three other phrases are useless clichés.

The Skills You'll Use

The Mathematics Test assesses your abiltty to solve mathematical problems by using

- basic and advanced high school math skills
- logical insight in problem-solving situations
- mathematical reasoning

You also need to understand basic mathematical terminology, principles, and formulas.

Your Mathematics Test Score

You have a total of 60 minutes to complete 60 items. The total Mathematics Test is scored from 1 to 36, with a mean score of 18. In addition to the total Mathematics Test score, three subscores are reported in the following areas.

- pre-algebra/elementary algebra (24 items)
- intermediate algebra/coordinate geometry (18 items)
- plane geometry/trigonometry (18 items)

The subscores range from 1 to 18, with a mean of 9.

The Level of Difficulty

The math section is slightly graduated in difficulty. That is, the easiest questions are at the beginning and the more difficult ones at the end. Keep in mind that *easy* and *difficult* are relative terms. What's easy for you may be, for example, difficult for your friend or vice versa. But generally, the first questions are the easiest and the last questions are the most difficult.

Using Your Calculator

The ACT allows the use of calculators for the Mathematics Test, and the American College Testing Program (the people who sponsor the exam) recommends that each test taker bring a calculator to the test. Even though no question will require the use of a calculator—that is, each question can be answered without one—in some instances, using a calculator will save you valuable time.

You should

- Bring your own calculator, since you can't borrow one during the exam.

- Bring a calculator even if you don't think you'll use it.

- Make sure that you're familiar with the use of your calculator.

- Make sure that your calculator has new, fresh batteries and is in good working order.

- Practice using your calculator on some of the problems to see when and where it will be helpful.

- Check for a shortcut in any problem that seems to involve much computation. But use your calculator if it will be time effective. If there appears to be too much computation or the problem seems impossible without the calculator, you're probably doing something wrong.

- Before doing an operation, check the number that you keyed in on the display to make sure that you keyed in the right number. You may wish to check each number as you key it in.

- Before using your calculator, set up the problem and/or steps on your paper. Write the numbers on paper as you perform each step on your calculator. (It is generally safer not to use the memory function on your calculator.)

- Be sure to carefully clear the calculator before beginning new calculations.

Be careful that you

- Don't rush out and buy a sophisticated calculator for the test.

- Don't bring a calculator that you're unfamiliar with.

- Don't bring a pocket organizer, hand-held mini-computer, laptop computer, or calculator with a typewriter-type keypad or paper tape.

- Don't bring a calculator that requires an outlet or any other external power source.

- Don't bring a calculator that makes noise.

- Don't try to share a calculator.

- Don't try to use a calculator on every problem.

- Don't become dependent on your calculator.

Take advantage of being allowed to use a calculator on the test. Learn to use your calculator efficiently by practicing. As you approach a problem, first focus on how to solve that problem, and then decide if the calculator will be helpful. Remember, a calculator can save you time on some problems, but also remember that each problem can be solved without one. Also remember that a calculator won't solve a problem for you by itself. You must understand the problem first.

The Directions

After solving each problem, choose the correct answer and fill in the corresponding space on your answer sheet. Do not spend too much time on any one problem. Solve as many problems as you can and return to the others if time permits. You are allowed to use a calculator on this test.

Note: Unless it is otherwise stated, you can assume all of the following:

1. Figures are NOT necessarily drawn to scale.

2. Geometric figures lie in a plane.

3. The word "line" means a straight line.

4. The word "average" refers to the arithmetic mean.

The Mathematics Test is different from the other three in that each question has five answer choices (**A, B, C, D, E** or **F, G, H, J, K**) rather than four.

The Types of Mathematics Questions

The mathematics questions may be based on any of these subject areas.

- pre-algebra
- elementary algebra
- intermediate algebra
- coordinate geometry
- plane geometry
- trigonometry

The following graph and table show the general breakdown of the mathematics questions by category.

Types of Mathematics Questions

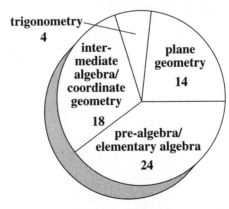

60 Total Items

MATHEMATICS CONTENT AREA BREAKDOWN
(approximate percentages)

Content	Number of Items	Percentages
Pre-algebra/ Elementary algebra	24	40%
Intermediate algebra/ Coordinate geometry	18	30%
Plane geometry	14	23%
Trigonometry	4	7%
Total	60	

Samples and Key Strategies for the Mathematics Questions

- Underline or circle what you're looking for.

- Simplify the problem.

- Work forward.

- Work backward, from the answers.

- Plug in simple numbers.

- Pull out information.

- Mark in, or fill in, the diagram.

- If no diagram is given, draw one.

- Use 10 or 100.

- Approximate.

- Glance at the choices on procedure problems.

- Be reasonable.

Underline or circle what you're looking for. Take advantage of being allowed to mark in the test booklet by always underlining or circling what you're looking for so you're sure that you're answering the right question.

Sample:

1. If $2x + 12 = 26$, then $x + 6 = ?$
   A. 7
   B. 13
   C. 14
   D. 19
   E. 38

You should first underline or circle "$x + 6$" because that's what you're solving for. Focusing on $x + 6$ may give you the insight to simply divide the complete equation by 2, giving you $x + 6 = 13$. This is the fastest method, but if you don't spot the shortcut, you could solve for x and then add 6. If you solve for x, you would first subtract 12 from each side.

$$\begin{array}{rcl} 2x + 12 & = & 26 \\ -12 & & -12 \\ \hline 2x & = & 14 \end{array}$$

Dividing each side by 2 gives $x = 7$.

At this point, you could easily select the most common wrong answer, choice **A**. But since you underlined $x + 6$, you're reminded to add 6 to your answer, giving you the correct answer of 13, choice **B**. *Make sure that you're answering the right question.*

Simplify the problem. Sometimes, combining terms, performing simple operations, or simplifying the problem in some other way will give you insight and make the problem easier to solve.

Sample:

2. If $x = -3$ and $y = 4$, then $xy^2 + 3x^2y + 4xy^2 + 2x^2y=?$

   F.   −420
   G.   −60
   H.   60
   J.   420
   K. 4,500

Simplifying this problem means first adding the like terms $(xy^2 + 4xy^2)$ and $(3x^2y + 2x^2y)$. After simplifying this problem to $5xy^2 + 5x^2y$, plug in the value -3 for x and 4 for y, which gives you

$$5(-3)(4)^2 + 5(-3)^2(4) = 5(-3)(16) + 5(9)(4)$$
$$= -15(16) + 45(4)$$
$$= -240 + 180$$
$$= -60$$

The correct answer is −60, choice **G.**

Work forward. If you immediately recognize the method or proper formula to solve the problem, then do the work. Work forward.

Sample:

3. $|-8 + 6| + |-7| = ?$

    A. 21
    B.   9
    C.   7
    D. −7
    E. −21

You should work this problem straight through as follows.

$$|-8 + 6| + |-7| = |-2| + |-7|$$
$$= 2 + 7$$
$$= 9$$

Notice that a quick look at the answer choices would let you eliminate choices **D** and **E,** since they are negative. If you add two absolute values, the answer can't be negative. Choice **B** is the correct answer.

Work backward, from the answers. If you don't immediately recognize a method or formula, or if using the method or formula would take a great deal of time, try working backward—from the answers. Since the answers are usually given in ascending or descending order, always start by plugging in the middle answer choice first if values are given. Then you'll know whether to go up or down with your next try. (Sometimes you might want to plug in one of the simple answers first.)

Sample:

4. Which of the following is a value of r for which $r^2 - r - 20 = 0$?

   F. 4
   G. 5
   H. 6
   J. 7
   K. 8

You should first underline or circle "value of r." If you've forgotten how to solve this equation, work backward by plugging in answers. Start with choice **H;** plug in 6.

$$(6)^2 - 6 - 20 \overset{?}{=} 0$$
$$36 - 6 - 20 \overset{?}{=} 0$$
$$30 - 20 \overset{?}{=} 0$$
$$10 \neq 0$$

Since this answer is too large, try choice **G,** a smaller number. Plugging in 5 gives

$$(5)^2 - 5 - 20 \overset{?}{=} 0$$
$$25 - 5 - 20 \overset{?}{=} 0$$
$$20 - 20 \overset{?}{=} 0$$
$$0 = 0$$

which is true, so **G** is the correct answer. *Working from the answers is a valuable technique.*

You could also work this problem by factoring into

$$(r-5)(r+4)0 = 0$$

and then setting $(r-5) = 0$ and $(r+4) = 0$, leaving $r = 5$ or $r = -4$.

Plug in simple numbers. Substituting numbers for variables can often help in understanding a problem. Remember to plug in *simple, small* numbers, since you have to do the work.

Sample:

5. If s and t represent integers, and $s < t$ and $s > 0$, then which of the following must be true?

   A. $t < 0$
   B. $t > 1$
   C. $s - t > 0$
   D. $s > t$
   E. $t < s$

Since the question says "s and t represent integers, and $s < t$ and $s > 0$," substitute 1 for s and 2 for t. In this question, you should underline or circle "must be true" because that's what you're looking for. So as you plug in for s and t, you can stop when you get an answer that must be true.

   A. $t < 0$ *but* $2 \nless 0$ *(false)*
   B. $t > 1$ *and* $2 > 1$ *(must be true)*

Since choice **B** must be true, it's the correct answer, and you can stop here.

Notice that when a choice is false, there's no need to try other possible numbers. But if a choice is true, you should try a few other possibilities to make sure that you can see that it works in all cases. In this case, it's easy to say that it would always be true.

The other choices would look like this.

C. $s - t > 0$, $1 - 2 > 0$ *but* $-1 \not> 0$ *(false)*
D. $s > t$ *but* $1 \not> 2$ *(false)*
E. $t < s$ *but* $2 \not< 1$ *(false)*

Pull out information. Pulling information out of the word problem structure can often give you a better look at what you're working with; therefore, you gain additional insight into the problem.

Sample:

6. A professor gives a 5-point quiz to her class. A 4 is scored by 40 of the students, a 3 is scored by 30 students, and a 2 is scored by 30 students. No students scored 1 or 5. What is the average score on this quiz?

    F. 1.0
    G. 1.6
    H. 3.1
    J. 3.4
    K. 4.0

You should first underline or circle "average score on this quiz?" Now, pulling out information gives you the following:

4—40

3—30

2—30

So to work this problem, you should first multiply

$$4 \times 40 = 160$$

$$3 \times 30 = 90$$

$$2 \times 30 = 60$$

Then add the outcomes: $160 + 90 + 60$ gives 310.

Now divide by the number of students, which is 100, that is, $(40 + 30 + 30 = 100)$ to get the average.

$$310 / 100 = 3.1$$

Choice **H** is the correct answer.

Mark in, or fill in, the diagram. Marking in diagrams as you read the questions can save you valuable time. Marking can also give you insight into how to solve a problem because you'll have the complete picture clearly in front of you.

Sample:

7. In the isosceles triangle below, $\overline{AB} = \overline{BC}$, and $\angle x$ is 55°. What is the measure of $\angle z$?

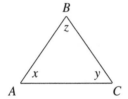

A. 10°
B. 20°
C. 40°
D. 70°
E. 85°

First underline or circle what you're looking for, "$\angle z$." (You may want to circle it in the diagram as well.) Next, in the isosceles triangle, immediately mark in that $\overline{AB}$ and $\overline{BC}$ are equal. Then mark in $\angle x$ as 55° Since $\overline{AB} = \overline{BC}$, then $\angle x = \angle y$ (angles opposite equal sides are equal) and $x + y = 110°$ After you mark in the information, your diagram should look like this.

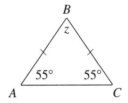

Since there are 180° in a triangle, simply subtract 180 – 110, leaving 70. So ∠z = 70°, choice **D**.

If no diagram is given, draw one. Sketching diagrams or simple pictures can also be helpful in problem solving because the diagram may tip you off to either a simple solution or a method for solving the problem.

Sample:

8. The sides of a triangle are 60, 80, and 100 inches long. What is the measure of the angle between the two shortest sides?

   F. 60°
   G. 90°
   H. 95°
   J. 100°
   K. 120°

   First underline or circle the words "angle between the two shortest sides." Now draw a triangle and label each segment of the triangle, with the shortest side across from the smallest angle and the largest side across from the largest angle.

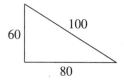

Drawing and labeling the triangle should help you determine
that the sides 60–80–100 are in the ratio 6–8–10, or 3–4–5.
Because this is a Pythagorean triple, the angle between the two
shortest sides must be 90°. Remember, the Pythagorean theorem
works only with right triangles. So the correct choice is **G.**

Use 10 or 100. Some problems may deal with percent or percent
change. If you don't see a simple method for working the problem,
try using values of 10 or 100 and see what you get.

Sample:

9. If 40% of the students in a class have blue eyes and 20% of those
with blue eyes have brown hair, then what percent of the original total number have brown hair and blue eyes?

    A.   4%
    B.   8%
    C. 16%
    D. 20%
    E. 32%

First underline or circle "percent of the original total number . . . brown hair . . . blue eyes." In this problem, if you don't spot a simple method, try starting with 100 students in the class. Since 40% of them have blue eyes, then 40 students have blue eyes. Now, the problem says that 20% of those students with blue eyes have brown hair. So take 20% of 40, which gives you

$$.20 \times 40 = 8$$

Since the question asks what percent of the original total number have blue eyes and brown hair, and since you started with 100 students, the answer is choice **B,** 8 out of 100, or 8%.

Approximate. If it appears that extensive calculations are going to be necessary to solve a problem, check to see how far apart the choices are and then approximate. The reason for checking the answers first is to give you a guide to see how freely you can approximate.

Sample:

10. Sam's promotion earns him a new salary that is an increase of 11% of his present salary. If his present salary is $39,400 per year, what is his new salary?

    F. $39,411
    G. $39,790
    H. $43,734
    J. $49,309
    K. $53,912

First underline or circle "new salary." Notice that except for the first two choices, the answers are spread out. Approximate 11% as 10% and $39,400 as $40,000. Now a quick second look tells you that choices **F** and **G** aren't sensible because if you add 10% of $40,000, you get $44,000—eliminate choices **F** and **G**. Choice **H** is the only answer that's close to $44,000, and it is the correct answer. Since you're allowed to use a calculator on this test, this problem would be easy to check (or work) with the calculator if the answer choices were close together.

Glance at the choices on procedure problems. Some problems may not ask you to solve for a numerical answer or even an answer including variables. Rather, you may be asked to set up the equation or expression without doing any solving. A quick glance at the answer choices will help you know what is expected.

Sample:

11. Uli was 12 years old x years ago. In 8 years, how old will she be?

    A. $20 - x$
    B. $(12 + x) + 8$
    C. $(12 - x) + 8$
    D. $(8 + x) - 12$
    E. $(12 + 8) - x$

First underline or circle "In 8 years, how old." Next glance at the answers. Notice that none of them gives an actual numerical answer but rather each sets up a way to find the answer. Now set up the problem.

"12 years old x years ago" can be written as

$$12 + x$$

"In 8 years" tells you to add 8 more, so the answer is

$$(12 + x) + 8$$

which is choice **B.**

Be reasonable. Sometimes a reasonable approach will save you time or help you eliminate wrong answers that result from common mistakes. If no mathematical method comes to mind, try a reasonable approach. Also, after solving, always check to see that the answer is actually reasonable.

Sample:

12. Will can complete a job in 30 minutes. Eli can complete the same job in 60 minutes. If they work together, approximately how many minutes will it take them to complete the job?

   F. 90
   G. 60
   H. 45
   J. 30
   K. 20

First underline or circle "work together, approximately how many minutes." In a reasonable approach, you'd reason that since Will can complete the job alone in 30 minutes, then if he receives any help, the job should take less than 30 minutes. He's receiving a fair amount of help, so the answer must be well below 30 minutes. The only answer below 30 is choice **K** 20.

The Skills You'll Use

The Reading Test assesses your ability to

- understand
- interpret
- analyze

prose drawn from reading passages.

Your Reading Test Score

You have a total of 35 minutes to complete 4 reading passages and the 10 questions that follow each passage, a total of 40 questions. The Reading Test is scored from 1 to 36, with a mean score of 18. In addition to the total Reading Test score, two subscores are reported in the following areas.

- arts/literature (prose fiction, humanities—20 items)
- social studies/sciences (social studies, natural sciences—20 items)

The subscores range from 1 to 18, with a mean of 9.

The Directions

Each of the four passages in this test is followed by questions. Read the passage and choose the best answer to each question. Return to the passage as often as necessary to answer the questions.

The Types of Reading Passages

The Reading Test passages are drawn from

- prose fiction: excerpts from short stories or novels
- humanities: architecture, art, dance, music, philosophy, theater
- social studies: anthropology, economics, history, political science, psychology, sociology
- natural sciences: biology, chemistry, physical science, physics

The questions test your reading and reasoning abilities, not your prior knowledge of a subject or knowledge of vocabulary or rules of logic. The following graph and table show the general breakdown of the reading questions by category.

Types of Reading Questions

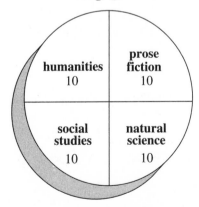

40 Total Items

READING CONTENT AREA BREAKDOWN *(approximate percentages)*		
Content	**Number of Items**	**Percentages**
Prose fiction	10	25%
Humanities	10	25%
Social studies	10	25%
Natural sciences	10	25%
Total	40	

The category of each passage is identified, and the lines of each passage are numbered.

The Types of Reading Questions

The majority of the Reading Test questions require careful thinking and reasoning, not just a basic understanding of the passage. Common types of questions ask you

- about the main idea, main point, purpose, or possible title of the passage

- about important details or information that is directly stated in the passage

- about the meaning of a word or phrase in a passage

- about information that is assumed, implied, or suggested or that can be reasonably inferred

- to recognize an author's point of view

- to make comparisons between ideas or characters

- to identify cause-effect relationships

- to make generalizations

CLIFFS QUICK REVIEW

Sample Passages, Questions, and Key Strategies for the Reading Questions

- Read the passage actively, marking the main points and other items you feel are important.

- Preread a few questions. Prereading can give you a clue about the passage and what to look for.

- Read the passage looking for its main point and structure.

- Make sure that your answer is supported by the passage.

- As you read, note the purpose or tone of the passage or portions of the passage.

- Make sure that the answer you select "answers the question." Some good or true answers are not correct.

- Take advantage of the line numbers.

- Read all the choices, since you're looking for the *best* answer given.

- Use an elimination strategy.

Read the passage actively, marking the main points and other items you feel are important. You can mark a passage by underlining or circling important information. But be sure you don't overmark, or you'll defeat the purpose of the technique. The following passage shows one way a test taker might mark a passage to assist in understanding the information given and to quickly return to particular information in the passage when necessary. You may find that circling works better for you or using other marks that you personally find helpful.

Sample passage:

Social science: This passage is from *The Russian Revolution* by Alan Moorehead (© 1958 by Time Inc.).

The <u>war</u> had put a fearful <u>strain upon the Czarist system</u>, and <u>Nicholas II</u> was no Peter the Great to set things right again. It was really a race now to see which would come first: the ending of the war or the revolution. There was always a chance,

5 of course, that the <u>revolution might be staved off</u> indefinitely provided that the <u>war ended soon</u> and victoriously; but in <u>December, 1916,</u> there was <u>no sign of this</u>. The Franco-British effort to break through the Dardanelles and come to the aid of their Russian allies had ended in disaster. The United States

10 had not yet come into the war. France was hanging on desperately in the winter mud at Verdun, and at sea the Germans were about to launch their U-boat campaign, which was designed to starve Britain into surrender. Something like 160 Austrian and German divisions were now entrenched along

15 the Russian front.

The <u>war</u>, then, as far as <u>Russia was concerned</u>, had subsided into a <u>despairing stalemate</u>. And yet, despite all this, it was <u>difficult to see where the revolution was going to come from</u>. A palace revolution, a rising of the <u>nobles</u> to replace the Czar,

20 was quite feasible; but <u>no single man</u> either in Petrograd or among the generals in the army <u>looked like being the leader</u> of such a movement. Then too, there existed among the liberals as well as among the aristocracy an <u>instinctive fear of</u> what might happen if they upset the throne, if the <u>illiterate masses,</u>

25 the "<u>Dark People</u>," followed their lead and raised a rebellion in the streets. Once let loose the mob and anything could happen; then all of them from <u>aristocrats to shopkeepers might be swept away</u>.

As for the left-wing revolutionary parties—the people who would accept rebellion at any cost—they too had been weakened by the war and driven underground. Most of the leaders were living in exile abroad or in Siberia: Lenin was in Switzerland, Trotsky was on his way to New York, Plekhanov, Axelrod, Martov, Dan, and many others were scattered through Europe; and most of them were quarreling bitterly among themselves. None of them were planning to return to Russia, none had any idea that revolution was at hand. Lenin was even saying at this time that he did not believe he would ever live to see it.

And so a strange apathy rests over the scene, and it is something of a marvel that the Russian revolution, the most important political event of modern times, the event which has done more to shape our lives than anything else, should have entered in such an unexpected and rudderless way into history. It seems almost to have come in, as it were, by the back door, and although it was so much talked about beforehand, it appears to have taken most of the main protagonists by surprise.

One has an entertaining glimpse of just how surprising the whole thing was from *Whitaker's Almanack,* the British reference book which has been issuing the vital statistics about the countries of the world year by year since the middle of the nineteenth century. In the volume dealing with 1916 everything is in order, and in its place, in the Russian section; the Czar is on his throne, the Duma is sitting, the imports and the exports are listed along with the figures dealing with the rainfall and the average extremes of temperature. But then in the next volume there is a sudden bewildered hiatus. In rather a shocked tone *Whitaker* reports that the Czar has been replaced by an M. Kerensky. "The newly-born freedom of the country," the book goes on, "has not up to the present proved an unmixed blessing as several opposing parties have arisen rendering any form of settled administration impossible." A certain "A. Oulianof Lenin" is believed to have seized the reins of power, and a "subaltern" has been named as commander-

in-chief. Worse still, "the army is in a state of <u>chaos</u> and the allies are dispatching no more material aid to Russia." The note ends, "Any <u>news</u> coming to hand <u>under the ruling conditions</u> must obviously be looked on with the <u>greatest</u>
70 <u>suspicion</u>."

Preread a few questions. Prereading can give you a clue about the passage and what to look for. Quickly reading a few of the questions before reading the passage may be very helpful, especially if the passage seems difficult or unfamiliar to you. *In prereading, read only the questions and NOT the answer choices* (which aren't included in the examples below). Notice that you should mark (underline or circle) what the question is asking. After you read the passage, you'll go on to read the questions again and each of their answer choices. The following questions give examples of ways to mark as you preread.

1. Which one of the following lines best states the <u>main point</u> of the passage?

The words *main point* are marked here. You should always read for the main point, but prereading this question is a good reminder.

2. It can reasonably be <u>inferred</u> from the <u>first paragraph</u> of the passage that:

Notice that *inferred* and *first paragraph* are marked. To answer this question, you'll need to draw information from the first paragraph by "reading between the lines."

5. From the context of the passage, the _Duma (line 55)_ is most likely:

Notice that _Duma (line 55)_ is marked. The marking helps you pinpoint where the answer can be found and makes you aware of looking for the meaning as the term is used in the passage.

7. According to the passage, in <u>late 1916</u>, the <u>leaders of the revolutionary parties</u> in Russia were:

Notice that _late 1916_ and _leaders of the revolutionary parties_ are marked. You'll need to focus on specific details to answer this question.

After such prereading and marking of the questions, you should go back and read the passage actively. The passage is reprinted below without the marking. Try marking it yourself this time before you go on to the sample questions that follow.

Social science: This passage is from _The Russian Revolution_ by Alan Moorehead (© 1958 by Time Inc.).

The war had put a fearful strain upon the Czarist system, and Nicholas II was no Peter the Great to set things right again. It was really a race now to see which would come first: the ending of the war or the revolution. There was always a chance,
5   of course, that the revolution might be staved off indefinitely provided that the war ended soon and victoriously; but in December, 1916, there was no sign of this. The Franco-British effort to break through the Dardanelles and come to the aid of their Russian allies had ended in disaster. The United States
10   had not yet come into the war. France was hanging on desperately in the winter mud at Verdun, and at sea the Germans were about to launch their U-boat campaign, which was designed to starve Britain into surrender. Something like 160 Austrian and German divisions were now entrenched along
15   the Russian front.

The war, then, as far as Russia was concerned, had subsided into a despairing stalemate. And yet, despite all this, it was difficult to see where the revolution was going to come from. A palace revolution, a rising of the nobles to replace the Czar,
20　was quite feasible; but no single man either in Petrograd or among the generals in the army looked like being the leader of such a movement. Then too, there existed among the liberals as well as among the aristocracy an instinctive fear of what might happen if they upset the throne, if the illiterate masses,
25　the "Dark People," followed their lead and raised a rebellion in the streets. Once let loose the mob and anything could happen; then all of them from aristocrats to shopkeepers might be swept away.

As for the left-wing revolutionary parties—the people who
30　would accept rebellion at any cost—they too had been weakened by the war and driven underground. Most of the leaders were living in exile abroad or in Siberia: Lenin was in Switzerland, Trotsky was on his way to New York, Plekhanov, Axelrod, Martov, Dan, and many others were scattered
35　through Europe; and most of them were quarreling bitterly among themselves. None of them were planning to return to Russia, none had any idea that revolution was at hand. Lenin was even saying at this time that he did not believe he would ever live to see it.
40　And so a strange apathy rests over the scene, and it is something of a marvel that the Russian revolution, the most important political event of modern times, the event which has done more to shape our lives than anything else, should have entered in such an unexpected and rudderless way into history.
45　It seems almost to have come in, as it were, by the back door, and although it was so much talked about beforehand, it appears to have taken most of the main protagonists by surprise.

One has an entertaining glimpse of just how surprising the
50　whole thing was from *Whitaker's Almanack,* the British reference book which has been issuing the vital statistics about the countries of the world year by year since the middle of the

nineteenth century. In the volume dealing with 1916 everything is in order, and in its place, in the Russian section; the
55 Czar is on his throne, the Duma is sitting, the imports and the
exports are listed along with the figures dealing with the rainfall and the average extremes of temperature. But then in the
next volume there is a sudden bewildered hiatus. In rather a
shocked tone *Whitaker* reports that the Czar has been replaced
60 by an M. Kerensky. "The newly-born freedom of the country,"
the book goes on, "has not up to the present proved an
unmixed blessing as several opposing parties have arisen rendering any form of settled administration impossible." A certain "A. Oulianof Lenin" is believed to have seized the reins
65 of power, and a "subaltern" has been named as commander-
in-chief. Worse still, "the army is in a state of chaos and the
allies are dispatching no more material aid to Russia." The
note ends, "Any news coming to hand under the ruling conditions must obviously be looked on with the greatest
70 suspicion."

Read the passage looking for its main point and structure. As you read the passage, try to focus on "what the author is really saying" or "what point the author is trying to make." There are many ways to ask about the main point of a passage.

Sample:

1. Which one of the following lines best states the main point of the passage?

   A. "The war, then, as far as Russia was concerned, had subsided into a despairing stalemate." (lines 16–17)

   B. "A palace revolution, a rising of the nobles to replace the Czar, was quite feasible; but no single man either in Petrograd or among the generals in the army looked like being the leader of such a movement." (lines 18–22)

   C. "None of them [that is, the revolutionary leaders] were planning to return to Russia, none had any idea that revolution was at hand." (lines 36–37)

   D. " . . . it is something of a marvel that the Russian revolution, the most important political event of modern times, the event which has done more to shape our lives than anything else, should have entered in such an unexpected and rudderless way into history." (lines 40–44)

   Throughout the passage, the suggestion is that although Russia was ripe for revolution, its occurrence in 1917 was a surprise. So choice **D** is the best answer. Choice **A** covers only one aspect of the passage—the status of the war. Choice **B** covers only the nobility and **C** only the revolutionary leaders. Therefore, these choices are incomplete as statements of the main idea.

Make sure that your answer is supported by the passage. Every single correct answer is in the passage or can be directly inferred from the passage.

Sample:

2. It can reasonably be inferred from the first paragraph of the passage (lines 1–15) that:

   F. in late 1916, Czarist Russia was dealing with internal problems rather than devoting itself to the war effort.
   G. the French and English had become disenchanted with Russia's war effort.
   H. if the United States had entered the war sooner, the Russian revolution wouldn't have occurred.
   J. at the end of 1916, the Germans appeared to have the upper hand in the war.

The best choice is **J,** which is supported by several details in the paragraph (for example, the Franco-British failure at the Dardanelles, the French plight at Verdun, the imminent German U-boat campaign, and the Austrian and German troops on the Russian front). There is no indication that the Czar is focusing on internal affairs, choice **F,** and there is no evidence that the French and English are disenchanted with Russia at this point, choice **G.** Choice **H** might at first appear to be a good choice, but the inference that the United States could have prevented the Russian revolution by entering the war earlier is simplistic, and it is not implied by the passage.

As you read, note the purpose or tone of the passage or portions of the passage. The structure and the words that the author uses to describe events, people, or places will help give you an understanding of for what specific purpose the author is writing or how the author wants you to feel or think.

Sample:

3. The purpose of the last paragraph of the passage (lines 49–70) is to:

   A. summarize the problems in prerevolutionary Russia.
   B. suggest that the Allies planned to intervene in Russia.
   C. illustrate that the timing of the revolution came as a surprise.
   D. present the widely held view that Lenin was a vicious man and the power behind the revolution.

A question concerning purpose or tone may be based on the whole passage or a part of the passage, as is the case here. The best choice is **C** (lines 49-53). The first sentence is the paragraph's topic sentence. This paragraph isn't a summary, choice **A;** it's an example that supports the author's point. Also, although the paragraph mentions Lenin's position, choice **D,** nothing in the tone suggests that he was viewed as vicious. The paragraph quotes the *Almanack* as saying that news about Russia must be *looked on with the greatest suspicion* because of the country's unsettled state; the paragraph does *not* state that the Allies had plans to intervene, however, choice **B.**

Make sure that the answer you select "answers the question." Some good or true answers are not correct. Even though more than one choice may be true, you're looking for the *best* answer to the *question given.*

Sample:

4. According to the passage, the mood in Russia in December 1916 could best be described as:

   F. angry.
   G. contentious.
   H. apathetic.
   J. philosophical.

It might seem reasonable to think that people who will soon stage a revolution would be *angry,* choice **F** (why would they rebel, you might wonder, if they weren't). But *according to the passage* (see line 17), Russians weren't as angry at that point (December 1916) as they were discouraged. So choice **H,** *apathetic* (showing little emotion or interest) is the best choice. Choice **G** would be a good, true answer if the question were about the revolutionary leaders, who are said to be *quarreling bitterly.* But the question asks about the mood in Russia as a whole, not only among the revolutionaries. Choice **J** indicates a calm and reflective mood that isn't indicated in the passage.

Take advantage of the line numbers. All passages have the lines numbered, which, in questions that mention specific line numbers, gives you the advantage of being able to quickly spot where the information is located. Once you spot the location, be sure to read the line(s) before and after the lines mentioned. This nearby text can be very helpful in putting the information in the proper context and answering the question.

Sample:

5. From the context of the passage, the *Duma* (line 55) is most likely:

    F. a parliament.
    G. a conspirator against the Czar.
    H. an underground revolutionary organization.
    J. the government-sponsored newspaper.

The clue here is the verb in the sentence—*is sitting,* which rules out choices **G, J,** and even **H** because *sit* in a context such as this generally refers to meetings of official groups. Choices **G** and **H** are also eliminated because the phrase *the Duma is sitting* is used as an example of the fact that, according to the *Almanack,* everything was in order in 1916 Russia. It's unlikely that either a conspiracy or meetings of an underground organization would be evidence of the stability of the status quo. Choice **F** is the correct answer.

Read all the choices, since you're looking for the *best* answer given. *Best* is a relative term; that is, determining what is *best* may mean choosing from degrees of *good, better,* or *best*. Although you may have more than one good choice, you're looking for the **best** of those given. Remember, the answer doesn't have to be perfect, just the best of those presented to you. So don't get stuck on one choice before you read the rest.

Sample:

6. Which of the following is the best explanation for the term *Dark People* used in line 25?

   F. The poor in Russia were unintelligent and prone to violence.
   G. Those in the masses were dark skinned, while most Russian nobles were fair skinned.
   H. The poor in Russia were involved in the occult and in witch-craft.
   J. To the aristocracy, the poor were a great unknown and vaguely sinister.

It's possible that out of context choices **F, G,** and **H** could be explanations for the term *Dark People,* as *Dark* could conceivably refer to violence or to skin color or to the occult, but the passage doesn't link the term to any of these possibilities. Also, choice **F** is incorrect because the masses are referred to as *illiterate,* which is not synonymous with *unintelligent*. The *best* choice is **J,** which is supported by the mention of the fear that if the mob were to rise, the aristocrats might be *swept away,* a possibility that would suggest that the poor masses were both *unknown* and *vaguely sinister.*

Use an elimination strategy. Often you can arrive at the right answer by eliminating other answers. Watch for key words in the answer choices to help you find the main point given in each choice. Notice that some incorrect choices are too general, too specific, irrelevant, or off topic or that they contradict information given in the passage.

Sample:

7. According to the passage, in late 1916 the leaders of the revolutionary parties in Russia were: ·

   A. in the Russian army and scattered throughout Europe.
   B. pessimistic about the possibility of an imminent revolution.
   C. unwilling to take the chance that a revolution at that time would go too far and ruin the country.
   D. waiting for a major victory in the war before starting the revolution.

   You can eliminate choice **A.** Although the revolutionary leaders were scattered throughout Europe, nothing suggests that they were in the *army*. You can eliminate choice **C** because it applies to the nobles, not the revolutionaries. You can eliminate choice **D** because the revolutionary leaders would have no reason to wait for a major victory, since a major victory could only strengthen the Czar's position. You're left with choice **B,** the correct choice (see lines 29-39).

Three Final Strategies

If you're having real trouble with a passage or simply running out of time, try one of these three strategies.

Skip a difficult passage. You could skip a difficult passage entirely, along with the questions based on it, and come back to them later. Remember that you can return to those questions only while you're working in the Reading Test. Also, if you use this strategy, take care to mark your answers in the correct spaces on the answer sheet when you skip a group of questions.

Skim the passage. If you're running out of time, you might want to skim the passage and then answer the questions—referring back to the passage when necessary.

Potshot questions and spots in the passage. For this "*last resort* method," if questions on a passage refer to line numbers and you have only a few minutes left (and haven't yet read a passage), simply read the questions that refer to specific lines in the passage and read only those specific lines in the passage (potshot them) to try to answer the question. This final strategy may help you at least eliminate some answer choices and add one or two right answers to your score. And always remember to put down at least a guess answer for all questions.

The Skills You'll Use

The Science Reasoning Test assesses your ability to

- understand
- interpret
- analyze
- evaluate
- reason
- problem solve

from passages, figures, and tables containing scientific information.

Your Science Reasoning Test Score

You have a total of 35 minutes to complete 7 separate sets of information containing a total of 40 questions. The Science Reasoning Test is scored from 1 to 36, with a mean score of 18.

The Directions

Each of the 7 passages in this test is followed by several questions. After you read each passage, select the correct choice for each of the questions that follow the passage. Refer to the passage as often as necessary to answer the questions. You may NOT use a calculator on this test.

(Note that each set of scientific information is called a *passage*.)

The Types of Science Reasoning Passages

The Science Reasoning Test consists of three types of passages.

- data representation: information presented in tables, and/or figures (including graphs)

- research summaries: information from studies or experiments described with the aid of tables, and/or figures (including graphs)

- conflicting viewpoints: information concerning the different theories, viewpoints, or hypotheses of two or more scientists concerning a subject or scientific question

The following graph and table show the number of questions and percentages for each type of passage.

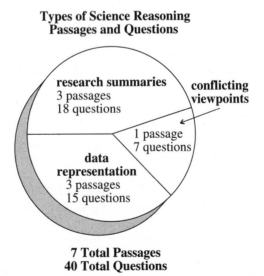

**Types of Science Reasoning
Passages and Questions**

research summaries
3 passages
18 questions

**conflicting
viewpoints**

1 passage
7 questions

**data
representation**
3 passages
15 questions

**7 Total Passages
40 Total Questions**

SCIENCE REASONING CONTENT AREA BREAKDOWN *(approximate percentages)*		
Content	**Number of Items**	**Percentages**
Data representation	15	38%
Research summaries	18	45%
Conflicting viewpoints	7	17%
Total	40	

The Science Categories

The content of the passages in the Science Reasoning Test comes from courses commonly taught in grades 7 through 12 (and possibly first-year college). The emphasis of this test is science reasoning skills, not recall of scientific content or general science knowledge. The passages come from the following categories.

- biology

- earth/space sciences

- chemistry

- physics

Some knowledge of scientific terms and basic facts may be helpful in understanding the passages and answering questions, but you don't need an advanced knowledge of the subjects. Remember, this is a science "reasoning" test.

The use of calculators is NOT permitted on the Science Reasoning Test, although some basic arithmetic computations may be necessary for some of the questions.

General Strategies for Any Science Reasoning Test Question

- Work quickly. Since you have 7 passages and 40 questions to complete in 35 minutes, *you must work quickly*. You have about 5 minutes for each passage and group of questions that follow. Spend about 2 minutes making sure you understand the passage (including the text and any graphic material) and about 20 to 30 seconds on each question.

- Actively read the information given. Mark the main points and other items you feel are important (such as similarities or differences in theories or studies).

- Actively read the questions, focusing on key words. Make sure you're answering the right question or looking at the right table or figure.

- Preread a few questions. Sometimes taking a quick look at a few questions (but not the answer choices) can be helpful before you look at the passage.

- Read all the choices, since you're looking for the *best* answer given. Although you may have more than one good choice, you're looking for the best of all choices. So don't get stuck rereading one choice before you read the others.

- Use an elimination strategy. You can often arrive at the right answer by eliminating other answers. Watch for things that are wrong with answer choices.

- Don't be overwhelmed by the amount of information given. Even though it may appear that you've been given a great deal of information (for example, text plus three or four tables and figures) for some questions, look at how the information is organized and focus on where each question leads you.

Sample Passages, Questions, and Key Strategies for Data Representation Questions

- Focus on understanding what information is given. Review any additional information given (descriptive paragraphs, headings, scale factors, legends, and so forth).

- Don't memorize the information; refer back to the tables or figures.

- Perform basic calculations, when needed, using the information.

- Reason from the information given.

- Look for obvious large changes (high points, low points, trends, large numbers, small numbers, and so forth).

- Work with the information given.

- Draw conclusions, form hypotheses, and make predictions.

Sample passage:

Recent research indicates that Precambrian Time started about 4.5 billion years ago and was composed of three eras—Azoic, Archeozoic, and Proterozoic. Following the Precambrian Time came the Paleozoic Era (beginning 600 million years ago), the Mesozoic Era (beginning 225 million years ago), and the Cenozoic Era (beginning 65 million years ago). Figure 1 and Tables 1 though 3 give information about these periods.

began 4.5 billion years ago	began 600 million years ago	began 225 million years ago	began 65 million years ago

Era: Azoic, Archeozoic,   Paleozoic   Mesozoic   Cenozoic
      Proterozoic
      (Precambrian Time)

Figure 1

Table 1		
Paleozoic Era		
Period (from earliest)	Length of time (in millions of years)	Development of life (examples)
Cambrian	120	trilobites
Ordovician	45	mollusks
Silurian	30	eurypterids
Devonian	60	fish
Mississippian	35	amphibians, insects
Pennsylvanian	35	early reptiles
Permian	50	seed plants

Table 2		
Mesozoic Era		
Period (from earliest)	Length of time (in millions of years)	Development of life (examples)
Triassic	45	dinosaurs
Jurassic	50	birds
Cretaceous	65	flowering plants

Table 3		
Cenozoic Era		
Period or epoch (from earliest)	Length of time (in years)	Development of life (examples)
Tertiary Period	63,000,000	
Paleocene Epoch	10,000,000	small mammals
Eocene Epoch	15,000,000	fruits, grasses, monkeys
Oligocene Epoch	14,000,000	early elephants, horses
Miocene Epoch	12,000,000	apes
Pliocene Epoch	12,000,000	primitive human beings
Quaternary Period	2,010,000	
Pleistocene Epoch	2,000,000	modern humans
Holocene Epoch	10,000	cultivated plants, tamed animals

Focus on understanding what information is given. Review any additional information given (descriptive paragraphs, headings, scale factors, legends, and so forth). Examining the table or figure to see how it organizes the information is the key to understanding what information is given.

Sample:

1. On the basis of the information in Figure 1, which of the following must be true?

   A. The Paleozoic Era was longer than the Azoic and Archeozoic Eras combined.
   B. The Proterozoic Era was shorter than the Azoic Era.
   C. The Mesozoic Era was shorter than the Proterozoic Era.
   D. The Paleozoic Era was longer than the Mesozoic Era.

Figure 1 shows that the Paleozoic Era began 600 million years ago and lasted until the Mesozoic Era, which began 225 million years ago. So the Paleozoic Era was 375 million years long (600 − 225). The Mesozoic Era lasted until the Cenozoic Era, which began 65 million years ago. So the Mesozoic Era lasted 160 million years (225 − 65). Therefore the Paleozoic Era must have been longer than the Mesozoic Era, and choice **D** is the correct answer. Note that you're not given enough information about the Azoic, Archeozoic, or Proterozoic Eras to make any comparisons between or determinations concerning their lengths.

Don't memorize the information; refer back to the tables or figures. Since you're allowed to look back at the information given, don't attempt to memorize the information. Instead, notice how many tables or figures there are, what each one refers to, and which one you should focus on for a particular question.

Sample:

2. The Mesozoic Era was known as the Age of Reptiles. Based on the information in Table 1 and Table 2, all of the following could be true about this era EXCEPT:

   F. during the Jurassic Period, dinosaurs reached their largest size.

   G. dinosaurs first appeared in the Triassic Period.

   H. dinosaurs died at the end of the Cretaceous Period.

   J. reptiles first appeared at the beginning of the Triassic Period.

First notice that you should focus on Table 1 and Table 2. Don't memorize the information in the tables, simply refer to it. Also, be sure to underline or circle the word *EXCEPT* to make sure that you answer the right question. Table 2, which gives information on the Mesozoic Era, doesn't mention reptiles as a group (only the dinosaurs). Table 1, however, does tell you that early reptiles first appeared toward the latter part of the Paleozoic Era. So they couldn't have first appeared in the Mesozoic Era. Choice **J** is the correct answer.

Perform basic calculations, when needed, using the information. Although you may not use a calculator on this section, you will some-times need to do basic calculations. Such calculations shouldn't be extensive.

Sample:

3. Based on the information in Table 1, oysters could have appeared approximately how many millions of years before snakes?

    A.   35
    B.   65
    C. 135
    D. 255

The total number of years between mollusks (oysters) and early reptiles (snakes) was approximately 135 million years (30 + 60 + 35 = 125). The number 125 is only a possibility rather than a certainty because the oysters could have developed up to 45 mil-lion years earlier, and the snakes could have developed up to 35 million years later. But the only answer in the range of 125 mil-lion to 205 million is choice **C,** 135 million.

Reason from the information given. Since this is a test of science reasoning ability, you should be able to make logical connections and deductions from the information.

Sample:

4. The Mississippian and Pennsylvanian Periods are often called the Carboniferous Period. Using the information given, which one of the following could be a possible reason for the name "Carboniferous"?

   F. Great coal deposits were formed.
   G. Fruits and grasses developed.
   H. Seed plants produced carbon as they died.
   J. Dinosaurs gave off carbon dioxide.

By a process of elimination you could reason that the period was named the Carboniferous Period because great coal deposits were formed. Choice **F** is the correct answer. Choices **G, H,** and **J** all refer to developments of life *after* the Mississippian and Pennsylvanian Periods.

Look for obvious large changes (high points, low points, trends, large numbers, small numbers, and so forth). Usually "obvious" items are easy to spot, but sometimes they take a more careful second look before they become apparent.

Sample:

5. Prior to the Quaternary Period, the period of the shortest duration produced the first air-breathing animal. According to the information given, which of the following could be the name of this animal?

   A. Turtle
   B. Frog
   C. Trilobite
   D. Eurypterid

First, look for the shortest period prior to the Quaternary Period. To find it will take a second look through all three tables, which will identify the period as the Silurian (Table 1). Only eurypterids, choice **D,** are listed as developing at this time and are therefore the only possible choice as the first air-breathing animals.

Work with the information given. Sometimes, approximating can make the work easier, especially if the question asks for an approximation or if the answers are far apart.

Sample:

6. Modern humans appeared about how many millions of years after the first dinosaurs appeared?

   F. 115
   G. 170
   H. 220
   J. 260

The question asks "*about* how many millions of years." Noticing how much room you have between the choices will help you determine how accurate you should be. Since dinosaurs first developed in the Triassic Period, which was followed by the Jurassic, Cretaceous, and Tertiary Periods, all came before modern humans first appeared, which was about 200 million years (choice **H**) (45 + 50 + 65 + 63 = 223).

Draw conclusions, form hypotheses, and make predictions. Focusing on the question and any new information given will help you use your reasoning ability.

Sample:

7. Near the end of the Pleistocene Epoch, mammoths and woolly rhinos became extinct, yet other large mammals of the time, such as whales and elephants, are living today. Which of the following is the most logical reason that mammoths and woolly rhinos became extinct nearly 2 million years ago?

   A. Shortage of food for larger animals
   B. Inability to adapt to changing conditions
   C. Inability to withstand cold temperatures
   D. Aggression of natural enemies

Given the choices, the most logical is the inability to adapt to changing conditions. Choice **B** is the correct answer. Since other large animals, some that are known to have survived, would also have been subject to shortage of food, choice **A,** and cold temperatures, choice **C,** those two answers are not logical. There is no information on which to evaluate the aggression of natural enemies, choice **D.**

Sample Passages, Questions, and Key Strategies for Research Summary Questions

- Focus on the purpose of the study or experiment(s), their differences, similarities, and outcomes, and how many were completed.

- Consider possible hypotheses or generalizations that can be made from the results.

- Watch for the methods used and the design of each study or experiment.

- Notice what may be suggested by the evidence or outcome and how the data were obtained and kept.

- Understand how the data are displayed (table and/or figure).

- Reason from the information and draw conclusions.

Sample passage:

Buckeye caterpillars take and store certain chemicals such as iridoid glycosides from their host plants. Wolf spiders prey upon buckeye caterpillars for food. Scientists have noted that these spiders prefer some buckeye caterpillars to others. They hypothesize that spiders have taste preferences that vary according to which plants the caterpillars eat.

In order to determine whether wolf spiders find buckeye caterpillars that store iridoid glycosides unpalatable (not pleasing to taste), two experiments were conducted—one in the field and one in the laboratory. For both experiments, two types of caterpillars were used—those reared on *Plantago lanceolata* (containing very high levels of iridoid glycosides) and those raised on *P. major* (containing very low levels of iridoid glycosides).

Experiment 1—In the Field

Spiders were located in the field at night by headlamp and were randomly offered either a buckeye caterpillar raised on *P. lanceolata* or a buckeye caterpillar raised on *P. major*. Figure 1 compares the acceptability of these two types of caterpillars to the spiders.

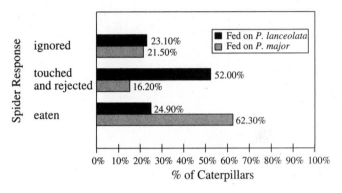

Figure 1

Experiment 2—In the Lab

This experiment was conducted with 50 spiders collected in the field. Ten trials were conducted per spider. Every third day for approximately one month, two buckeye caterpillars were offered to each spider—one caterpillar raised on *P. lanceolata* and one raised on *P. major*—and spider responses were recorded. Figure 2 shows percentage of caterpillars eaten, and Figure 3 shows spider response, where higher values indicate greater acceptability of the caterpillar to the spider.

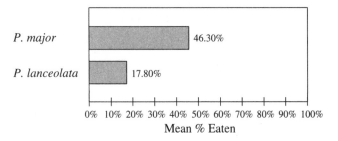

Figure 2

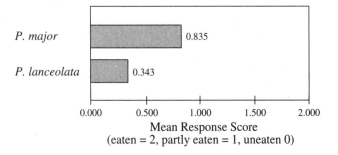

Figure 3

Focus on the purpose of the study or experiment(s), their differences, similarities, and outcomes, and how many were completed. You may wish to underline or circle similarities and/or differences in the studies and outcomes.

Sample:

8. How is the design of Experiment 1 different from the design of Experiment 2?

   F. In Experiment 1, trials give spiders no choice, whereas in Experiment 2, trials give spiders a choice.
   G. In Experiment 1, trials give spiders a choice, whereas in Experiment 2, trials give spiders no choice.
   H. In Experiment 1, spider responses are examined, whereas in Experiment 2 caterpillar responses are examined.
   J. In Experiment 1, caterpillar fates are examined, whereas in Experiment 2, spider fates are examined.

As you focus on each experiment in this passage, you should notice or mark the differences. In Experiment 1, field spiders weren't given a choice when presented with caterpillars for food. In Experiment 2, lab spiders were presented with a choice between caterpillars fed on *P. major* and caterpillars fed on *P. lanceolata.* So choice **F** is correct.

Consider possible hypotheses or generalizations that can be made from the results. Here you should consider important data and how the information relates to the results of each experiment.

Sample:

9. On the basis of the experimental results, one can generalize that which of the following is responsible for protecting buckeye caterpillars from being eaten by wolf spiders?

   A. Bitter-tasting chemicals in certain plants
   B. Sour-tasting chemicals in certain plants
   C. *P. major*
   D. Iridoid glycosides in the caterpillars

Three of the answer choices are very similar, so you should take care to choose the answer that is the most specific and directly related to material in the passage. Since the data indicate that spiders ate significantly more *P. major*-reared caterpillars, choice **C** is incorrect. Of the remaining three possible answers, choice **D** is the only one that is supported by information in the passage and is therefore the correct answer.

Watch for the methods used and the design of each study or experiment. In some cases, scientists make an assumption in setting up an experiment or study. Focusing on the methods and design will help you understand what is being assumed.

Sample:

10. All of the following are unstated assumptions of the experimental design EXCEPT:

    F. wolf spiders make distinctions between caterpillars based on taste.

    G. wolf spiders avoid caterpillars that do not taste good to them.

    H. iridoid glycosides are nontoxic (not poisonous) to wolf spiders.

    J. iridoid glycosides are nontoxic (not poisonous) to buckeye caterpillars.

The experimental design does *not* assume that iridoid glycosides are nontoxic to wolf spiders, choice **H**. If it were so assumed, then the scientists would not have expected that spiders would consistently reject caterpillars raised on plants high in this chemical (which was the case).

Notice what may be suggested by the evidence or outcome and how the data were obtained and kept. Carefully following what actually happened in the experiments will help you spot what this evidence suggests.

Sample:

11. During the course of this study, four spiders died in the laboratory. All four of these spiders had eaten only caterpillars reared on *P. lanceolata.* This evidence may suggest that:

    A. iridoid glycosides are poisonous to wolf spiders.
    B. iridoid glycosides are poisonous to buckeye caterpillars.
    C. *P. lanceolata* is eaten by wolf spiders.
    D. *P. lanceolata* is poisonous to buckeye caterpillars.

Wolf spiders don't directly eat *P. lanceolata* (choice **C**). Instead, they eat caterpillars that store chemicals that are found in this plant. Four spiders that were fed *only* caterpillars high in iridoid glycosides died, which suggests that this chemical may be harmful, and even fatal, to wolf spiders. Choice **A** is the correct answer.

Understand how the data are displayed (table and/or figure).
How well you understand the method of display can be a major factor in how well you understand the information and outcome. Make sure you understand what the graphically displayed material tells you.

Sample:

12. During the course of Experiment 1, some of the caterpillars offered to spiders in the field were released by the spiders after being touched but not yet bitten. This particular behavior may suggest that the spider's detection of a harmful chemical in its prey is:

    F. restricted to tasting the chemical.
    G. not restricted to tasting the chemical.
    H. restricted to touching the chemical.
    J. not restricted to touching the chemical.

    Notice how Figure 1 displays the information. This information (and the information in this question) indicates that spiders may, using the sense of touch, be sensitive to the presence of harmful chemicals in their prey (touch-and-reject). Spider responses of taste-and-reject (indicated by partly eaten caterpillars, as shown in Figure 3) may indicate detection of a harmful chemical by taste. So choices **F** and **H** are incorrect. While both choices **G** and **J** are suggested by the experiments, of the choices given, this *particular behavior* (caterpillars released after being touched but not yet bitten) suggests only choice **G,** which is the correct answer.

Reason from the information and draw conclusions. You must sometimes be able to draw a logical conclusion from the information presented, a conclusion not provided for you in the data. But be sure that the conclusion is *logically based* on the data.

Sample:

13. Which of the following conclusions about the relationship between caterpillar diet and caterpillar interactions with wolf spiders would be consistent with the results of the two experiments?

    A. Wolf spiders prefer buckeye caterpillars that have been raised on a diet of *P. lanceolata.*

    B. Wolf spiders prefer only large buckeye caterpillars that have been raised on a diet of *P. major.*

    C. Buckeye caterpillars fed on plants low in iridoid glycosides were preferred by wolf spiders to those fed on plants high in iridoid glycosides.

    D. Buckeye caterpillars fed on plants high in iridoid glycosides were preferred by wolf spiders to those fed on plants low in iridoid glycosides.

For this question, arriving at a logical conclusion based on the data may be best accomplished by a process of elimination. The data clearly indicate that spiders don't prefer caterpillars that have been raised on plants high in iridoid glycosides. So choices **A** and **D** are incorrect. There are two problems with choice **B.** The word *only* is too broad. It could not be determined from these experiments that the spiders have no *other* food preferences (in normal circumstances in the wild, for example). Also, nothing in the data concerns the size of the caterpillars preferred, and this choice indicates a preference for *large* caterpillars. Be careful you don't assume things not based on information given. The best choice here is **C.**

Sample Passages, Questions, and Key Strategies for Conflicting Viewpoints Questions

- Understand the topic and basic premise of each viewpoint, theory, or hypothesis.

- Identify the reasoning involved in the viewpoints and extend that reasoning to other logical conclusions based on it.

- Be aware of what might strengthen or weaken a viewpoint.

- Analyze the specifics of each viewpoint and the argument supporting it.

- Mark the differences and similarities in the viewpoints.

- Look for what might be suggested or implied by an argument.

- Reason from new information.

Sample passage:

Various theories have arisen to explain why the earth's protective ozone layer has been depleted. Following are just three such theories that might explain the phenomenon.

Theory 1

The overall global warming of our planet is primarily responsible for the dissipation of the protective ozone layer in our upper atmosphere. The huge amounts of air pollutants, such as nitrous oxide and sulfur oxide gases, from factories and automobiles have caused the greenhouse effect, which causes a general global warming. Ozone (O_3), which normally resides in an upper atmospheric layer, is heated by this greenhouse effect. In turn, it rises, thinning out as it does so because it has a greater and greater surface area to cover as it moves farther from the earth. The phenomenon is similar to the thinning out of a balloon's surface material as it is inflated. The natural mechanism for replenishing this layer does not keep up with this thinning effect, as surface area is proportional to the square of the radius, so the layer appears thin and depleted.

Theory 2

The thinning of our planet's protective ozone layer is just another natural occurrence, resulting from the periodic reversal of the magnetic poles of our planet. From the geologic record, it is known that the earth's magnetic field has reversed itself at least 150 times in its history. The core of the earth, which contains a large amount of molten iron, is in constant flux, which causes the ongoing changes in the earth's planetary magnetic field. This ongoing, natural planetary magnetic field change, in turn, results in dramatic weather pattern variance, including wide swings in lightning frequency and strength. Lightning, of course, is directly responsible for the natural production of ozone. Lightning is known to strike diatomic oxygen molecules, breaking them into single oxygen atoms, called radicals, which quickly bond to other diatomic oxygen molecules to form triatomic ozone, O_3.

Theory 3

The relatively thin ozone layer in our upper atmosphere, which protects us from harmful ultraviolet radiation of the sun, is being depleted because human-produced chemicals interfere with the natural production cycle of ozone. Chlorofluorocarbons, or CFCs, found in many aerosol propellants and refrigerants introduce chlorine radicals into our upper atmosphere. These chlorine radicals bond with lone oxygen atoms, atoms produced by the action of lightning on oxygen molecules, atoms naturally destined to join with diatomic oxygen to form ozone, in our atmosphere. Thus our ozone layer is not replenished at an adequate rate, and the observed thinning results.

Understand the topic and basic premise of each viewpoint, theory, or hypothesis. As you read each viewpoint, theory, or hypothesis, focus on "what point the scientist is trying to make."

Sample:

14. The argument made in Theory 2 is based on all of the following EXCEPT:

   F. the earth's magnetic field is dynamic.
   G. lightning is responsible for splitting up oxygen molecules.
   H. ozone, O_3, is formed when O_2 joins with a lone oxygen radical.
   J. the changing frequency and strength of lightning is determined by the protective ozone layer.

First focus on Theory 2 and underline or circle the words *argument, based,* and *EXCEPT.* Choices **F, G,** and **H** are known facts and are stated as such in the passage. According to the passage, however, it is the changes in the magnetic field, not the ozone layer, that determine the frequency of lightning, so **J** is the correct answer.

Identify the reasoning involved in the viewpoints and extend that reasoning to other logical conclusions based on it. Understanding the main point and the line of reasoning is key to drawing a logical conclusion.

Sample:

15. A logical conclusion that can be drawn from Theory 3 is that:

    A. ultraviolet rays continue to bombard us from the sun.
    B. decreasing the use of CFCs would help stabilize the ozone layer.
    C. ozone is a very stable material.
    D. chlorine gas, Cl, is as harmful to the ozone layer as are lone chlorine radicals.

Always circle or underline the main point of each theory, viewpoint, or hypothesis. The main point of Theory 3 is that CFCs are the cause of the ozone layer's depletion. Therefore, the logical conclusion would be that decreasing the use of CFCs would help stabilize the ozone layer, choice **B.**

Be aware of what might strengthen or weaken a viewpoint.
You'll need to recognize what points could logically support an argument and those that could logically call it into question or that could be a valid criticism of it.

Sample:

16. All of the following, if true, would weaken the argument presented in Theory 1 EXCEPT:

    F. the temperature at the altitude of the ozone layer causes thermal expansion.

    G. the ozone layer does not thin out as it expands; all gases thicken and cool as they expand.

    H. ozone is a denser gas than the atmospheric oxygen and would tend to fall closer to the earth under the pull of the earth's gravity.

    J. the ultraviolet shielding that the ozone layer is responsible for contributes to the greenhouse effect.

First, circle or underline the words *weaken* and *EXCEPT*. Next, focus on Theory 1. Choices **G, H,** and **J** would weaken the argument because they contradict the assumptions made in Theory 1. The correct answer is choice **F** because it is the only point that would support the argument, by reinforcing the expansion theory.

Analyze the specifics of each viewpoint and the argument supporting it. As you analyze, try to look at each of the pieces of the argument and how they fit together.

Sample:

17. To test the hypothesis put forth in Theory 1, useful experiments would examine all of the following EXCEPT:

    A. the effects of nitrous oxide and sulfur oxide gases on the greenhouse effect.

    B. the effect of temperature on the formation of ozone.

    C. the density of the ozone at varying altitudes.

    D. whether ozone contributes to the greenhouse effect.

To know what "useful experiments would examine," you need to carefully analyze Theory 1. Again, note the word *EXCEPT.* From the information and argument made in Theory 1, choices **A, B,** and **C** are all relevant subjects for experiments. But ozone is *affected by* the greenhouse effect, not the other way around, so an experiment concerning ozone's contribution *to* the greenhouse effect would not be useful. Choice **D** is the correct answer.

Mark the differences and similarities in the viewpoints. Notice the conflicts and contradictions. As you read each viewpoint, focus on what points make it different from the others and what points make it the same as the others.

Sample:

18. Theories 1 and 3 are similar in that they both:

    F. blame the depletion of the ozone layer on chlorofluorocarbons.

    G. base their arguments on human interference.

    H. rely on the greenhouse effect as an explanation for the depletion of the ozone layer.

    J. discuss the effect of lightning on the ozone layer.

Theories 1 and 3 both base their arguments on human interference, choice **G.** Theory 1 concerns huge amounts of pollutants, and Theory 3 concerns human-produced chemicals.

Look for what might be suggested or implied by an argument. Even though something isn't directly stated, you may arrive at it by reasoning or "reading between the lines."

Sample:

19. Which of the theories imply that the depletion of the earth's protecting ozone layer CANNOT be stopped?

    I. Theory 1

    II. Theory 2

    III. Theory 3

    A. I only

    B. II only

    C. III only

    D. I, II, and III

Since Theories 1 and 3 blame the ozone depletion on human interference, it is reasonable to assume then that humans should be able to stop this interference. But Theory 2 is based on a natural, repeating occurrence that is seemingly impossible for humans to intervene in. Therefore, Theory 2 implies that ozone depletion cannot be stopped, and choice **B** is the correct answer.

Reason from new information. Sometimes new information, information not included in the passage, is introduced in a question. You'll need to apply this information and reason from it.

Sample:

20. If lightning is directly responsible for action on the oxygen molecules, as mentioned in Theories 2 and 3, and if the frequency and strength of the lightning is weakened, which of the following must also be true if Theory 3 is true?

    F. The greenhouse effect would be an even more plausible explanation for ozone depletion.

    G. Human-produced chemicals could not be responsible for the ozone depletion.

    H. The ozone layer would be depleted at an even faster rate.

    J. The surface area of the ozone layer would be proportional to the cube of its radius.

If the frequency and strength of lightning is weakened, less ozone is produced. If Theory 3 is true, less ozone is produced. If both are true, then the ozone layer would be depleted at an even faster rate, choice **H.**

PRACTICE TEST

ANSWER SHEET FOR THE PRACTICE TEST
(Remove This Sheet and Use It to Mark Your Answers)

English Test

1 Ⓐ Ⓑ Ⓒ Ⓓ	26 Ⓕ Ⓖ Ⓗ Ⓙ	51 Ⓐ Ⓑ Ⓒ Ⓓ
2 Ⓕ Ⓖ Ⓗ Ⓙ	27 Ⓐ Ⓑ Ⓒ Ⓓ	52 Ⓕ Ⓖ Ⓗ Ⓙ
3 Ⓐ Ⓑ Ⓒ Ⓓ	28 Ⓕ Ⓖ Ⓗ Ⓙ	53 Ⓐ Ⓑ Ⓒ Ⓓ
4 Ⓕ Ⓖ Ⓗ Ⓙ	29 Ⓐ Ⓑ Ⓒ Ⓓ	54 Ⓕ Ⓖ Ⓗ Ⓙ
5 Ⓐ Ⓑ Ⓒ Ⓓ	30 Ⓕ Ⓖ Ⓗ Ⓙ	55 Ⓐ Ⓑ Ⓒ Ⓓ
6 Ⓕ Ⓖ Ⓗ Ⓙ	31 Ⓐ Ⓑ Ⓒ Ⓓ	56 Ⓕ Ⓖ Ⓗ Ⓙ
7 Ⓐ Ⓑ Ⓒ Ⓓ	32 Ⓕ Ⓖ Ⓗ Ⓙ	57 Ⓐ Ⓑ Ⓒ Ⓓ
8 Ⓕ Ⓖ Ⓗ Ⓙ	33 Ⓐ Ⓑ Ⓒ Ⓓ	58 Ⓕ Ⓖ Ⓗ Ⓙ
9 Ⓐ Ⓑ Ⓒ Ⓓ	34 Ⓕ Ⓖ Ⓗ Ⓙ	59 Ⓐ Ⓑ Ⓒ Ⓓ
10 Ⓕ Ⓖ Ⓗ Ⓙ	35 Ⓐ Ⓑ Ⓒ Ⓓ	60 Ⓕ Ⓖ Ⓗ Ⓙ
11 Ⓐ Ⓑ Ⓒ Ⓓ	36 Ⓕ Ⓖ Ⓗ Ⓙ	61 Ⓐ Ⓑ Ⓒ Ⓓ
12 Ⓕ Ⓖ Ⓗ Ⓙ	37 Ⓐ Ⓑ Ⓒ Ⓓ	62 Ⓕ Ⓖ Ⓗ Ⓙ
13 Ⓐ Ⓑ Ⓒ Ⓓ	38 Ⓕ Ⓖ Ⓗ Ⓙ	63 Ⓐ Ⓑ Ⓒ Ⓓ
14 Ⓕ Ⓖ Ⓗ Ⓙ	39 Ⓐ Ⓑ Ⓒ Ⓓ	64 Ⓕ Ⓖ Ⓗ Ⓙ
15 Ⓐ Ⓑ Ⓒ Ⓓ	40 Ⓕ Ⓖ Ⓗ Ⓙ	65 Ⓐ Ⓑ Ⓒ Ⓓ
16 Ⓕ Ⓖ Ⓗ Ⓙ	41 Ⓐ Ⓑ Ⓒ Ⓓ	66 Ⓕ Ⓖ Ⓗ Ⓙ
17 Ⓐ Ⓑ Ⓒ Ⓓ	42 Ⓕ Ⓖ Ⓗ Ⓙ	67 Ⓐ Ⓑ Ⓒ Ⓓ
18 Ⓕ Ⓖ Ⓗ Ⓙ	43 Ⓐ Ⓑ Ⓒ Ⓓ	68 Ⓕ Ⓖ Ⓗ Ⓙ
19 Ⓐ Ⓑ Ⓒ Ⓓ	44 Ⓕ Ⓖ Ⓗ Ⓙ	69 Ⓐ Ⓑ Ⓒ Ⓓ
20 Ⓕ Ⓖ Ⓗ Ⓙ	45 Ⓐ Ⓑ Ⓒ Ⓓ	70 Ⓕ Ⓖ Ⓗ Ⓙ
21 Ⓐ Ⓑ Ⓒ Ⓓ	46 Ⓕ Ⓖ Ⓗ Ⓙ	71 Ⓐ Ⓑ Ⓒ Ⓓ
22 Ⓕ Ⓖ Ⓗ Ⓙ	47 Ⓐ Ⓑ Ⓒ Ⓓ	72 Ⓕ Ⓖ Ⓗ Ⓙ
23 Ⓐ Ⓑ Ⓒ Ⓓ	48 Ⓕ Ⓖ Ⓗ Ⓙ	73 Ⓐ Ⓑ Ⓒ Ⓓ
24 Ⓕ Ⓖ Ⓗ Ⓙ	49 Ⓐ Ⓑ Ⓒ Ⓓ	74 Ⓕ Ⓖ Ⓗ Ⓙ
25 Ⓐ Ⓑ Ⓒ Ⓓ	50 Ⓕ Ⓖ Ⓗ Ⓙ	75 Ⓐ Ⓑ Ⓒ Ⓓ

CUT HERE

ANSWER SHEET FOR THE PRACTICE TEST
(Remove This Sheet and Use It to Mark Your Answers)

Mathematics Test

1 Ⓐ Ⓑ Ⓒ Ⓓ Ⓔ	31 Ⓐ Ⓑ Ⓒ Ⓓ Ⓔ
2 Ⓕ Ⓖ Ⓗ Ⓙ Ⓚ	32 Ⓕ Ⓖ Ⓗ Ⓙ Ⓚ
3 Ⓐ Ⓑ Ⓒ Ⓓ Ⓔ	33 Ⓐ Ⓑ Ⓒ Ⓓ Ⓔ
4 Ⓕ Ⓖ Ⓗ Ⓙ Ⓚ	34 Ⓕ Ⓖ Ⓗ Ⓙ Ⓚ
5 Ⓐ Ⓑ Ⓒ Ⓓ Ⓔ	35 Ⓐ Ⓑ Ⓒ Ⓓ Ⓔ
6 Ⓕ Ⓖ Ⓗ Ⓙ Ⓚ	36 Ⓕ Ⓖ Ⓗ Ⓙ Ⓚ
7 Ⓐ Ⓑ Ⓒ Ⓓ Ⓔ	37 Ⓐ Ⓑ Ⓒ Ⓓ Ⓔ
8 Ⓕ Ⓖ Ⓗ Ⓙ Ⓚ	38 Ⓕ Ⓖ Ⓗ Ⓙ Ⓚ
9 Ⓐ Ⓑ Ⓒ Ⓓ Ⓔ	39 Ⓐ Ⓑ Ⓒ Ⓓ Ⓔ
10 Ⓕ Ⓖ Ⓗ Ⓙ Ⓚ	40 Ⓕ Ⓖ Ⓗ Ⓙ Ⓚ
11 Ⓐ Ⓑ Ⓒ Ⓓ Ⓔ	41 Ⓐ Ⓑ Ⓒ Ⓓ Ⓔ
12 Ⓕ Ⓖ Ⓗ Ⓙ Ⓚ	42 Ⓕ Ⓖ Ⓗ Ⓙ Ⓚ
13 Ⓐ Ⓑ Ⓒ Ⓓ Ⓔ	43 Ⓐ Ⓑ Ⓒ Ⓓ Ⓔ
14 Ⓕ Ⓖ Ⓗ Ⓙ Ⓚ	44 Ⓕ Ⓖ Ⓗ Ⓙ Ⓚ
15 Ⓐ Ⓑ Ⓒ Ⓓ Ⓔ	45 Ⓐ Ⓑ Ⓒ Ⓓ Ⓔ
16 Ⓕ Ⓖ Ⓗ Ⓙ Ⓚ	46 Ⓕ Ⓖ Ⓗ Ⓙ Ⓚ
17 Ⓐ Ⓑ Ⓒ Ⓓ Ⓔ	47 Ⓐ Ⓑ Ⓒ Ⓓ Ⓔ
18 Ⓕ Ⓖ Ⓗ Ⓙ Ⓚ	48 Ⓕ Ⓖ Ⓗ Ⓙ Ⓚ
19 Ⓐ Ⓑ Ⓒ Ⓓ Ⓔ	49 Ⓐ Ⓑ Ⓒ Ⓓ Ⓔ
20 Ⓕ Ⓖ Ⓗ Ⓙ Ⓚ	50 Ⓕ Ⓖ Ⓗ Ⓙ Ⓚ
21 Ⓐ Ⓑ Ⓒ Ⓓ Ⓔ	51 Ⓐ Ⓑ Ⓒ Ⓓ Ⓔ
22 Ⓕ Ⓖ Ⓗ Ⓙ Ⓚ	52 Ⓕ Ⓖ Ⓗ Ⓙ Ⓚ
23 Ⓐ Ⓑ Ⓒ Ⓓ Ⓔ	53 Ⓐ Ⓑ Ⓒ Ⓓ Ⓔ
24 Ⓕ Ⓖ Ⓗ Ⓙ Ⓚ	54 Ⓕ Ⓖ Ⓗ Ⓙ Ⓚ
25 Ⓐ Ⓑ Ⓒ Ⓓ Ⓔ	55 Ⓐ Ⓑ Ⓒ Ⓓ Ⓔ
26 Ⓕ Ⓖ Ⓗ Ⓙ Ⓚ	56 Ⓕ Ⓖ Ⓗ Ⓙ Ⓚ
27 Ⓐ Ⓑ Ⓒ Ⓓ Ⓔ	57 Ⓐ Ⓑ Ⓒ Ⓓ Ⓔ
28 Ⓕ Ⓖ Ⓗ Ⓙ Ⓚ	58 Ⓕ Ⓖ Ⓗ Ⓙ Ⓚ
29 Ⓐ Ⓑ Ⓒ Ⓓ Ⓔ	59 Ⓐ Ⓑ Ⓒ Ⓓ Ⓔ
30 Ⓕ Ⓖ Ⓗ Ⓙ Ⓚ	60 Ⓕ Ⓖ Ⓗ Ⓙ Ⓚ

CUT HERE

ANSWER SHEET FOR THE PRACTICE TEST
(Remove This Sheet and Use It to Mark Your Answers)

Reading Test

1 Ⓐ Ⓑ Ⓒ Ⓓ
2 Ⓕ Ⓖ Ⓗ Ⓙ
3 Ⓐ Ⓑ Ⓒ Ⓓ
4 Ⓕ Ⓖ Ⓗ Ⓙ
5 Ⓐ Ⓑ Ⓒ Ⓓ

6 Ⓕ Ⓖ Ⓗ Ⓙ
7 Ⓐ Ⓑ Ⓒ Ⓓ
8 Ⓕ Ⓖ Ⓗ Ⓙ
9 Ⓐ Ⓑ Ⓒ Ⓓ
10 Ⓕ Ⓖ Ⓗ Ⓙ

11 Ⓐ Ⓑ Ⓒ Ⓓ
12 Ⓕ Ⓖ Ⓗ Ⓙ
13 Ⓐ Ⓑ Ⓒ Ⓓ
14 Ⓕ Ⓖ Ⓗ Ⓙ
15 Ⓐ Ⓑ Ⓒ Ⓓ

16 Ⓕ Ⓖ Ⓗ Ⓙ
17 Ⓐ Ⓑ Ⓒ Ⓓ
18 Ⓕ Ⓖ Ⓗ Ⓙ
19 Ⓐ Ⓑ Ⓒ Ⓓ
20 Ⓕ Ⓖ Ⓗ Ⓙ

21 Ⓐ Ⓑ Ⓒ Ⓓ
22 Ⓕ Ⓖ Ⓗ Ⓙ
23 Ⓐ Ⓑ Ⓒ Ⓓ
24 Ⓕ Ⓖ Ⓗ Ⓙ
25 Ⓐ Ⓑ Ⓒ Ⓓ

26 Ⓕ Ⓖ Ⓗ Ⓙ
27 Ⓐ Ⓑ Ⓒ Ⓓ
28 Ⓕ Ⓖ Ⓗ Ⓙ
29 Ⓐ Ⓑ Ⓒ Ⓓ
30 Ⓕ Ⓖ Ⓗ Ⓙ

31 Ⓐ Ⓑ Ⓒ Ⓓ
32 Ⓕ Ⓖ Ⓗ Ⓙ
33 Ⓐ Ⓑ Ⓒ Ⓓ
34 Ⓕ Ⓖ Ⓗ Ⓙ
35 Ⓐ Ⓑ Ⓒ Ⓓ

36 Ⓕ Ⓖ Ⓗ Ⓙ
37 Ⓐ Ⓑ Ⓒ Ⓓ
38 Ⓕ Ⓖ Ⓗ Ⓙ
39 Ⓐ Ⓑ Ⓒ Ⓓ
40 Ⓕ Ⓖ Ⓗ Ⓙ

CUT HERE

ANSWER SHEET FOR THE PRACTICE TEST
(Remove This Sheet and Use It to Mark Your Answers)

Science Reasoning Test

1 ⒶⒷⒸⒹ	26 ⒻⒼⒽⒿ
2 ⒻⒼⒽⒿ	27 ⒶⒷⒸⒹ
3 ⒶⒷⒸⒹ	28 ⒻⒼⒽⒿ
4 ⒻⒼⒽⒿ	29 ⒶⒷⒸⒹ
5 ⒶⒷⒸⒹ	30 ⒻⒼⒽⒿ
6 ⒻⒼⒽⒿ	31 ⒶⒷⒸⒹ
7 ⒶⒷⒸⒹ	32 ⒻⒼⒽⒿ
8 ⒻⒼⒽⒿ	33 ⒶⒷⒸⒹ
9 ⒶⒷⒸⒹ	34 ⒻⒼⒽⒿ
10 ⒻⒼⒽⒿ	35 ⒶⒷⒸⒹ
11 ⒶⒷⒸⒹ	36 ⒻⒼⒽⒿ
12 ⒻⒼⒽⒿ	37 ⒶⒷⒸⒹ
13 ⒶⒷⒸⒹ	38 ⒻⒼⒽⒿ
14 ⒻⒼⒽⒿ	39 ⒶⒷⒸⒹ
15 ⒶⒷⒸⒹ	40 ⒻⒼⒽⒿ
16 ⒻⒼⒽⒿ	
17 ⒶⒷⒸⒹ	
18 ⒻⒼⒽⒿ	
19 ⒶⒷⒸⒹ	
20 ⒻⒼⒽⒿ	
21 ⒶⒷⒸⒹ	
22 ⒻⒼⒽⒿ	
23 ⒶⒷⒸⒹ	
24 ⒻⒼⒽⒿ	
25 ⒶⒷⒸⒹ	

--CUT HERE--

CLIFFS QUICK REVIEW

Time: 45 Minutes
75 Questions

DIRECTIONS

In the left-hand column, you will find passages in a "spread-out" format with various words and phrases underlined and numbered. In the right-hand column, you will find a set of responses corresponding to each underlined portion. If the underlined portion is correct standard written English, is most appropriate to the style and feeling of the passage, or best makes the intended statement, mark the letter indicating "NO CHANGE." If the underlined portion is not the best choice given, choose the one that is. For these questions, consider only the underlined portions; assume that the rest of the passage is correct as written. You will also see questions concerning parts of the passage or the whole passage. Choose the response you feel is best for these questions.

PASSAGE I

> The following paragraphs
> are given a number in brackets
> above each one. Items 14 and
> 15 ask you to make choices
> concerning the combination or
> deletion of certain paragraphs.

Jackie Robinson
[1]

Despite his enormous ability, Jackie Robinson did not begin to play major league baseball until he was twenty-eight. <u>In 1947, joining the</u> Brooklyn Dodgers as the first black player. He promptly won the Rookie of the Year award and within three years became the batting champion and the Most Valuable Player in the National League. <u>He was, observers agree</u> the most versatile player of his era

1. A. NO CHANGE
B. Joining, in 1947,
C. In 1947, he joined
D. He joined in 1947

2. F. NO CHANGE
G. He was, observers agree,
H. He was observers agree
J. He was observers agree,

<u>at that point in time.</u>

3. A. NO CHANGE
B. at that time.
C. then.
D. OMIT the underlined portion.

[2]

[1] As an undergraduate at
UCLA, Robinson in one year
<u>had won</u> varsity letters in four
4

4. F. NO CHANGE
G. winning
H. has won
J. won

different <u>sports; baseball, football,</u>
                                    5
basketball, and track. [2] He
was one year old when his
family moved from Georgia to
California.
[3] Robinson grew up in
Pasadena, where
his remarkable athletic
abilities thrived. [4] After
graduating from college, he
even won the ping-pong
championship when he
served in the Army in
World War II. 6

5. A. NO CHANGE
B. sports: baseball,
       football,
C. sports, baseball
       football,
D. sports baseball,
       football,

6. Which of the follow-
    ing sequences of sen-
    tences will make the
    development of this
    paragraph most clear?
    F. NO CHANGE
    G. 2, 1, 3, 4
    H. 2, 3, 1, 4
    J. 2, 3, 4, 1

[3]

Rachel Robinson, his wife is just as remarkable. Also a student at UCLA when they met, she supported him through the bleakest periods of his career. She raised their three children, continued her studies in graduate school, and eventually becoming a professor at the Yale School of Nursing. Since the death of her husband, she has managed the operations of the

Jackie Robinson Foundation. 9

7. **A.** NO CHANGE
   B. Rachel Robinson, his wife,
   C. His wife Rachel Robinson
   D. His wife Rachel Robinson,

8. **F.** NO CHANGE
   G. she eventually became a professor
   H. eventually became a professor
   J. eventually becomes

9. The writer wishes to add the detail that the Jackie Robinson Foundation has supported the college careers of over four hundred black students. Which of the following is the best way to incorporate this information?

A. Add a new paragraph of one sentence that reads: "The Jackie Robinson Foundation has supported the college careers of over four hundred black students."

B. Add a final sentence to the paragraph that reads: "The Jackie Robinson Foundation has supported the college careers of over four hundred black students."

C. Replace the final period with a comma and add the following: "which has supported the college careers of over four hundred black students."

D. Replace the final period with a comma and add the following: "which has, in accordance with its purpose and function, supported more than four hundred black college students in their academic endeavors."

[4]

When his baseball career had ended, Jackie Robinson entered the business world and rose to the vice presidency of a large coffee company.

10. **F.** NO CHANGE
    G. was ending,
    H. ends,
    J. came to its completion,

On the other hand, he wrote a sports column for a New York

11. **A.** NO CHANGE
    B. In addition,
    C. Nevertheless,
    D. However,

newspaper, appeared on a weekly
radio program, and was active in the
N.A.A.C.P.

[5]

After his retirement,
his attendance was rare at a
baseball game. Many expected he
would one day enter politics, but
he never really became an
important political figure. He was,
however, a leader of two of the
earliest civil rights marches and an
ally of Martin Luther King. His
baseball achievements were never
forgotten, in 1962 he was elected
to the Baseball Hall of Fame.

12. **F.** NO CHANGE
    G. rarely attending a
    baseball game.
    H. he rarely attends a
    baseball game.
    J. he rarely attended a
    baseball game.

13. **A.** NO CHANGE
    B. forgotten; in 1962
    C. forgotten, and as a
    result in 1962
    D. forgotten. So that
    in 1962

Items 14 and 15 pose questions about the essay as a
whole.

14. Suppose that you wished to make this a four-paragraph instead of a five-paragraph essay. Which two paragraphs could best be combined?

F. Paragraphs 1 and 2

G. Paragraphs 2 and 3

H. Paragraphs 3 and 4

J. Paragraphs 4 and 5

15. Suppose that for reasons of space you were required to delete one of these five paragraphs. Which one of the following could be omitted with the least harm to the central focus of the essay?

A. Paragraph 2

B. Paragraph 3

C. Paragraph 4

D. Paragraph 5

PASSAGE II

Tomato Imports

In the last twenty years, tomato production in the United States has declined sharply; meanwhile imports have more than doubled. Much of the foreign crop arrives from Mexico, when the colder winters north of the Rio Grande make tomato growing

difficult and hard to do. But the seasonal imports are not the only problem for American growers.

The second-leading exporter is the Netherlands, with a climate as cold as Pennsylvania's. The Dutch grow their tomatoes in greenhouses and ship gourmet varieties to markets throughout the United States.

16. **F.** NO CHANGE
    G. sharply:
       meanwhile
    H. sharply,
       meanwhile
    J. sharply
       meanwhile

17. **A.** NO CHANGE
    B. difficult and hard.
    C. difficult to do.
    D. difficult.

18. **F.** NO CHANGE
    G. are
    H. was
    J. were

In California, one step growers are taking is <u>diversify.</u> In the past, most American growers offered only three kinds of

19. A. NO CHANGE
B. to diversify
C. they are diversifying
D. by diversification

<u>tomatoes: mature-greens, vine-ripened, and cherries.</u> Now markets often stock eight to ten kinds, and specialty stores handle as many as twenty. But the exotic new types

20. F. NO CHANGE
G. tomatoes; mature-greens, vine-ripened, and cherries.
H. tomatoes; mature-greens; vine-ripened; and cherries.
J. tomatoes— mature-greens vine-ripened, and cherries.

<u>accounts for</u> only five percent of

21. A. NO CHANGE
B. accounted for
C. account for
D. will account for

the tomatoes sold. 22

22. The writer wishes to
add a concluding sen-
tence to this paragraph.
Of the following, which
is the most effective?

   F. Some of the new
tomatoes are
orange or yellow,
not the traditional
red.

   G. Therefore, ninety-
five percent of the
tomatoes sold
must be the
mature-greens,
vine-ripened, and
cherries.

   H. This figure suggests that by
simply adding
new products,
American farmers
will not recapture
their lost markets.

   J. Farmers in the
other tomato-
producing states
may follow the ex-
ample of the Cal-
ifornia growers.

[1] In the past, the chief worry of tomato growers was finding a fruit that could stand up to shipping and still appear good looking. [2] The least of their concerns was taste. [3] Until recently, American seed developers concentrated on disease resistance, crop yield, and how long a tomato would keep. [4] Now, with the competition from abroad, growers and seedsmen are looking for flavor and color. [25]

23. A. NO CHANGE
    B. appear well-looking.
    C. look well.
    D. look good.

24. F. NO CHANGE
    G. when a tomato would begin to rot.
    H. not rotting.
    J. shelf-life.

25. The writer wishes to add the following detail to this paragraph:

    "Growers no longer need fear losing up to half of their larger and hardier harvests to diseases like verticillium wilt."

    After which sentence in this paragraph is the most logical place to insert this sentence?
    A. 1
    B. 2
    C. 3
    D. 4

Growers like to blame the disappointing taste of supermarket tomatoes on transportation. Commercial <u>tomatoes they say,</u> are [26] picked properly but then dumped into huge trucks, driven for miles to packing houses, packed, trucked again to supermarket warehouses, and <u>then they are trucked one last time to the stores.</u> No wonder a [27]

26. F. NO CHANGE
    G. tomatoes they say
    H. tomatoes, they say
    J. tomatoes, they say,

27. A. NO CHANGE
    B. then trucked one last time to the stores.
    C. then they truck them at last to the stores.
    D. then, at last, they are trucked to the stores.

perfect tomato in the field <u>is not a perfect tomato, marketwise!</u> [28]

Growing tomatoes on a trellis may be a solution—or part of one. Tomatoes are usually grown in clumps on the ground, but trellis-grown fruit

28. F. NO CHANGE
    G. is imperfect as a tomato when it reaches the market!
    H. is a dud in the market!
    J. is no longer wholly perfect in the market!

can be <u>tended more careful.</u>
Workers, ²⁹

29. **A.** NO CHANGE
    B. tended carefully.
    C. tended more
       carefully.
    D. tended most
       careful.

<u>which</u> can harvest ground-grown
₃₀
tomatoes only once, can pick
only the ripest fruit from trellised
plants and go through the same field
many times. These better looking
and better tasting tomatoes may
turn out to be part of the answer to
the competition from Europe.

30. **F.** NO CHANGE
    G. that
    H. who
    J. whom

Item 31 poses a question
about the essay as a whole.

31. Suppose this assignment called for an argumentative essay on a controversial topic that clearly presented the writer's point of view. Would this essay fulfill the assignment?

A. Yes, because in the controversy between American and foreign growers, the author is on the side of American farmers.

B. Yes, because the author presents both sides of the issue and offers more than one solution to the problems.

C. No, because the essay is not an argument and the topic is not really controversial.

D. No, because the author does not make his or her position in the argument clear enough.

PASSAGE III

Distance Learning

Based on the principle that learning can take place outside a classroom, <u>the students at the new Florida Gulf Coast University are offered</u> a wide choice of new kinds of classes. Some are given on weekends, some in off-campus

32. F. NO CHANGE
   G. the students at the new Florida Gulf Coast University may choose from
   H. students at the new Florida Gulf Coast University select from
   J. the new Florida Gulf Coast University offers students

locations, and <u>some on videotape or over the Internet.</u> Almost ten

33. A. NO CHANGE
   B. and some on video-tape and some over the Internet.
   C. and some are offered on video-tape or over the Internet.
   D. on videotape over the Internet.

percent of <u>this terms classes</u> will be
conducted electronically.³⁴ Many of
the students will never see the
campus.

The school has elected to
eliminate many things that people
expect to find in a university.
There are no dorms. There is no
football stadium. <u>Nonetheless,</u>
³⁵

<u>there is</u> no intercollegiate athletics.
³⁶
The average freshman is not an
eighteen-year-old just out of high
school, but a thirty-three-year-old
with fifteen years of work
experience. The president of the

34. F. NO CHANGE
    G. this term's classes
    H. this terms' classes
    J. classes, that will be
        given this term

35. A. NO CHANGE
    B. However,
    C. In fact,
    D. On the other hand,

36. F. NO CHANGE
    G. there are
    H. there was
    J. there were

student body is a grandmother. ᴣ⁊

37. The author is considering moving the first sentence of this paragraph to the end and beginning with what is now the second sentence. Would this change improve the paragraph?

A. Yes, since the final sentence will sum up the paragraph and help the reader to remember what it said.

B. Yes, since the final sentence will explain more clearly the relation of the random details in the rest of the paragraph.

C. No, because the first sentence is a topic sentence that makes clear that the details are the result of a specific college policy.

D. No, because if the sentence comes at the end, it is no longer relevant to the content of the paragraph.

Unlike the University of
Florida or Florida State, continuing
[38]

education—that is the education of
an older generation of students, is
[39]
the major focus of Florida Gulf
Coast. So is a commitment to environmental studies, and all under-
graduates must complete an
environmental education class. As
part of the environmental emphasis,
all visitors to the campus are

offered a tour of the nearby
Everglades. [40]

38. F. NO CHANGE
    G. Different from the
University of
Florida and Florida
State,
    H. Unlike other uni-
versities like
Florida and Florida
State,
    J. Unlike the educa-
tional policies at
Florida and Florida
State,

39. A. NO CHANGE
    B. education—that is
the education of an
older generation of
students—
    C. education—that is,
the education of an
older generation of
students—
    D. education, that is
the education of an
older generation of
students,

40. The author is considering adding the follow-
ing sentence at the end
of the paragraph:

"Within twenty miles of the campus, the visitor can enjoy the sight of some of Florida's most magnificent water birds."

Should this sentence be added to the paragraph?

F. Yes, because it will make this very factual essay more interesting to the general reader.

G. Yes, because the sentence adds specific details to the topic of the study of the environment.

H. No, because it is not closely related to the central issues of the paragraph or the essay as a whole.

J. No, because it does not make clear why the university is concerned with the environment instead of education.

The location of the university was chosen <u>for it's</u> easy accessibility to₄₁ a major highway. Since so many of the students will be part-timers, on-campus housing construction is not a high priority. <u>Although theyre will,</u> in time, be student dormitories on the campus,₄₂ most of the students will commute from the nearby cities of Naples and Fort Meyers. Parking will be no problem; the first completed construction project was a huge parking lot.

41. A. NO CHANGE
   B. for its'
   C. for its
   D. for their

42. F. NO CHANGE
   G. Although they're will,
   H. Although there will,
   J. Although their will,

The president of the new campus always refers to the students as <u>"clients"</u> and his mission is to offer them the₄₃ services they need most. The curriculum was constructed in response to the wishes of the nearby communities, <u>who have expressed</u> their₄₄

43. A. NO CHANGE
   B. "clients";
   C. "clients,"
   D. clients;

44. F. NO CHANGE
   G. which have expressed
   H. and they have expressed
   J. having expressed

Item 45 poses a question about the essay as a whole.

preferences in comprehensive surveys. Career-oriented fields like health-care and real estate will be taught at several off-campus sites throughout a five-county area. In a cyberspace age, Florida Gulf Coast University will test how well "distance learning" can work.

45. Which of the following sentences best sums up the content of this essay?

A. Florida Gulf Coast University is concentrating on career-oriented fields in accordance with the wishes of the nearby communities.

B. Unlike many other universities, Florida Gulf Coast is chiefly concerned with making off-campus education as important as its traditional course offerings.

C. Florida Gulf Coast University is unusual among schools in its emphasis on varied kinds of instruction for local students of all ages.

D. Florida Gulf Coast University is a pioneer in providing the teacherless classroom for its students.

PASSAGE IV

Coyote Wars

[1] As the twentieth century draws to a close, the coyote can be found <u>at this time</u> in forty-nine of the fifty states. [2] Thirty years ago, most of the coyote population

46. F. NO CHANGE
G. at the present
H. now
J. OMIT the under-lined portion.

<u>was confined in</u> the western states, but now they prowl from Maine to Florida, and increasingly in urban areas. [3] Their range has extended north as far as Alaska and south

47. A. NO CHANGE
B. were confined in
C. was confined to
D. were confined to

through almost all of Central
America. 48

48. The author wishes to
add more detail to this
paragraph. Which of the
following would be the
most effective addition?

F. Add after the
phrase "fifty
states" in Sentence
1: "but not in
Hawaii."

G. Add after the
phrase "western
states" in Sentence
2: "such as
Arizona and
Colorado."

H. Add after the
phrase "urban
areas" in Sentence
2: "where they
scavenge in gar-
bage cans and kill
domestic pets."

J. Add after the
phrase "Central
America" in
Sentence 3:
"where they are
now found in
Mexico and
Guatemala."

This population explosion has a number of causes <u>which have made it occur.</u>[49] The elimination of the <u>more</u>[49] powerful natural enemies of the coyote like the wolf has freed the smaller animal from competition. Traps and poisons that have killed the less resourceful coyotes leave the wiliest ones to breed <u>ever more cunning animals.</u>[50]

A strong dominant pair will prevent all the other members of a pack from breeding, but random poisoning may lead to much more breeding within a pack. <u>This, in turn,</u>[51] leads to the need to expand the range to provide for the increased number of cubs.

49. A. NO CHANGE
   B. which make it happen.
   C. that bring it about.
   D. OMIT the underlined portion.

50. F. NO CHANGE
   G. cunninger animals
   H. more cunning animals
   J. more animals

51. A. NO CHANGE
   B. On the other hand, it
   C. This increase, in turn,
   D. Consequently, it

In southwest Oregon, a single marauding <u>coyote it is said to have killed</u> more than seven hundred sheep before it was finally trapped

52. F. NO CHANGE
G. coyote, it is said, to have killed
H. coyote is said, to have killed
J. coyote is said to have killed

and destroyed <u>in three years.</u> Some ranchers have responded with a new weapon, a collar worn by sheep that contains the

53. A. NO CHANGE
B. (Move this phrase to follow the word *sheep.*)
C. (Move this phrase to follow the word *trapped.*)
D. OMIT the underlined portion.

<u>fiercely toxic</u> Compound 1080. Ranchers say the amount of the deadly poison is so small

54. F. NO CHANGE
G. fierce toxic
H. fierce and toxic
J. toxically fierce

<u>which causes</u> no threat to the

55. A. NO CHANGE
B. which cause
C. that cause
D. that it causes

<u>environment the</u> EPA has approved the use of the collars in several western states.

56. F. NO CHANGE
G. environment, the
H. environment. The
J. environment and the

<u>But</u> there is opposition from many environmental groups.
⁵⁷
They point to the cruelty of the coyotes' death, which can last from three to twelve hours. The dangerous Compound 1080 can kill innocent animals and poses a special threat to eagles. <u>Due to the fact that the collars</u> may find their way into stream beds,
⁵⁸
there is fear of the widespread killing of fish and fish-eating birds

and animals. <u>Coyotes have been known to eat fish.</u>
⁵⁹

Many observers of the coyote wars are not optimistic. They point out that Americans have been attempting to wipe out the coyote

57. A. NO CHANGE
  B. Although
  C. Despite the fact that
  D. In addition,

58. F. NO CHANGE
  G. As a result of the fact that collars
  H. Because collars
  J. Collars

59. A. NO CHANGE
  B. (Add parentheses around this sentence.)
  C. Coyotes are known to be fisheaters.
  D. OMIT the underlined portion.

for over a century ~~and more than~~
~~one hundred years,~~ often killing off
half of the population in limited
areas. But that leaves the smartest
animals to reproduce, and then the
smartest of the next generation,
and so on. Should we wonder that
the battle is <u>far from over?</u>

60. **F.** NO CHANGE
G. and for over one
hundred years
H. (and more than one
hundred years)
J. OMIT the under-
lined portion.

61. **A.** NO CHANGE
B. not over yet.
C. very far from being
finished?
D. unfinished.

PASSAGE V

1950s Modernism
[1]

Styles of domestic architecture
come and go, but one that has
continued to interest a small
number of discerning homeowners
is 1950s modernism. The houses
are usually described by such
words <u>as "pure" or "uncluttered" or</u>
<u>"clean."</u> Their appeal may be their

62. **F.** NO CHANGE
G. as pure or unclut-
tered or clean.
H. as "pure," or
"uncluttered" or
clean.
J. as "pure" or
"uncluttered," or
"clean."

looks <u>or, as some psychologists</u>
<u>suggest</u> it may be that owners are
nostalgic for the fifties, for a time

63. A. NO CHANGE
  B. or, as some
    psychologists sug-
    gest,
  C. or, as is suggested
    by some
    psychologists,
  D. or as is suggested
    by some
    psychologists,

<u>that is perceived being</u> more

64. F. NO CHANGE
  G. that is perceived as
    being
  H. that is, perceived
    as being
  J. that is

<u>confident and optimistic as the</u>
<u>present.</u>

65. A. NO CHANGE
  B. confident as the
    present.
  C. confident and opti-
    mistic than the
    present.
  D. confident and more
    optimistic than the
    present.

[2]

Most fifties modern houses
have an open plan with as few
interior walls as possible and an
enclosing structural skeleton of

wood or steel. <u>There is floor-to-ceiling sliding glass doors linking</u> the interior with a courtyard or a garden. Above all, the lines are

66. **F.** NO CHANGE
   G. With floor-to-ceiling glass doors linking
   H. There are floor-to-ceiling glass doors linking
   J. Floor-to-ceiling glass doors link

clean and <u>simple; as a rule, the roof is flat.</u>

67. **A.** NO CHANGE
   B. simple as a rule the roof is flat.
   C. simple, as a rule, the roof is flat.
   D. simple: as a rule, the roof is flat.

[3]

68

Formica and vinyl, <u>just coming into
general use in the fifties,</u>⁶⁹ are
employed widely, and even
unpainted plywood is popular.

68. Which of the following
would be the best open-
ing sentence for
Paragraph 3 to provide
an effective transition
from Paragraph 2 to
Paragraph 3?
  F. Some of the houses
  have large stone
  fireplaces.
  G. The houses were
  often built in
  groups of three or
  four, often on
  scenic wooded
  lots.
  H. Inside, the materials are often rela-
  tively cheap.
  J. Many of the
  houses have beau-
  tiful gardens.

69. A. NO CHANGE
  B. coming into gen-
  eral use just in the
  fifties
  C. in general use in
  the fifties
  D. generally used in
  the fifties

There are built-ins everywhere.
Beds fit into walls, seats are built-in,
and to assure an uncluttered floor
space, there are plenty of cupboards.

[4]

Many of the fifties modern
houses are built in wooded areas.
Some <u>are built</u> around a tree that
grows through the flat roof.
Others may have a pool that is
part of the living room. The most
spectacular example of this

70

70. The author is considering changing *are built*
to *are constructed*.
Which of the following
is the best reason for
making this revision?

F. The revision
avoids the awk-
ward use of the
passive verb.

G. The revision
avoids the repe-
tition of the verb
used in the pre-
ceding sentence.

H. Given a choice
between a short
and longer word
with the same
meaning, good
writers always use
the longer word.

J. The denotation of
the verb *con-
structed* is more
appropriate in this
context than that
of the verb *built*.

impulse <u>in Pennsylvania</u> is
probably Frank Lloyd Wright's [71]

71. The author wishes the reader to know that Wright built his house on a waterfall in Pennsylvania. To make this fact clear, which of the following is the best placement of the phrase *in Pennsylvania*?

   A. NO CHANGE

   B. (Move the prepositional phrase to the beginning of the sentence.)

   C. (Move the prepositional phrase to follow *example*.)

   D. (Move the prepositional phrase to the end of the sentence.)

house on a waterfall. 72

72. The author wishes to add the following sentence to this paragraph. Should it come at the beginning or at the end?

"Modernism attempts to integrate indoors and outdoors, to link people and the landscape."

F. At the beginning, because it provides a transition from Paragraph 3 and introduces the subject of Paragraph 4.

G. At the beginning, because it mentions *landscape* and the rest of the paragraph is about the out-of-doors.

H. At the end, where it will make a logical transition to the content of Paragraph 5.

J. At the end, where it will explain why Wright built the house on a waterfall.

[5]

Furnished with furniture by
Eames or sculpture by Noguchi,
and designed by architects like
Neutra or Schindler, <u>the end of the
war saw a small boom in the
construction of modern houses.</u>
These homes were expensive and

73. A. NO CHANGE
   B. a small construc-
      tion boom in mod-
      ern houses took
      place at the end of
      the war.
   C. modern houses
      enjoyed a small
      construction boom
      at the end of the
      war.
   D. there was a small
      boom in the con-
      struction of mod-
      ern houses at the
      end of the war.

never <u>approached, came near, or
challenged</u> the wild popularity of
the suburban ranch-house style.

74. F. NO CHANGE
   G. came near or
      approached
   H. either approached
      or came near
   J. approached

Within ten years, the modern style
was out of fashion altogether. The
simplicity that once attracted buyers
was now condemned as cold and
unwelcoming. But fifty years later,
a small but enthusiastic group is
eager to buy these houses and willing to pay very high prices for
them. 75

75. The final sentence is an
    appropriate closing to
    the essay because:
    A. it raises questions
       that invite further
       research.
    B. it explains why
       the architecture
       has enjoyed con-
       tinued popularity.
    C. it refers back to
       the idea that
       began the essay.
    D. it concludes the
       essay on a per-
       sonal note.

STOP. IF YOU FINISH BEFORE TIME IS UP, CHECK YOUR
WORK ON THIS SECTION ONLY. DO NOT WORK ON ANY
OTHER SECTION IN THE TEST.

Time: 60 Minutes
60 Questions

After solving each problem, choose the correct answer and fill in the corresponding space on your answer sheet. Do not spend too much time on any one problem. Solve as many problems as you can and return to the others if time permits. You are allowed to use a calculator on this test.

Note: Unless it is otherwise stated, you can assume all of the following:

1. Figures are NOT necessarily drawn to scale.

2. Geometric figures lie in a plane

3. The word "line" means a straight line.

4. The word "average" refers to the arithmetic mean.

1. Of the 40 graduating students in a class, 30% are math majors. How many students in this class are NOT math majors?

    A. 10
    B. 12
    C. 28
    D. 32
    E. 38

2. In the figure below, line ℓ_1 is parallel to line ℓ_2. What is the measure of x?

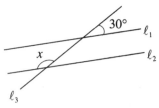

F. 30°
G. 60°
H. 120°
J. 150°
K. 175°

3. John's average on three tests is 80. If he scores 70 on the fourth test, what is his average for all four tests?

A. 72
B. 72.5
C. 77
D. 77.5
E. 79

4. If 30% of a mountain's height is 6,000 feet, what is 50% of the mountain's height, in feet?

F. 8,000
G. 9,000
H. 10,000
J. 12,000
K. 20,000

5. Point Q on a thermometer is midway between $-6°$ and $22°$. What is the reading of point Q?

A. $2°$
B. $8°$
C. $14°$
D. $16°$
E. $28°$

6. Square S and rectangle R have equal areas. The length of R is 4 times its width. What is the perimeter of R if the perimeter of S is 24?

F. 12
G. 24
H. 30
J. 36
K. 72

7. What is the value of $(p-8)$ if $(8-2p)=16$?

A. -20
B. -12
C. -4
D. 4
E. 8

8. If $abc \neq 0$, what is the value of $\dfrac{(-5a)^2(-3b^3)(2c^2)^3}{(25a^3)(-9b^2)(6c^5)}$?

F. $\dfrac{4bc}{9a}$

G. $\dfrac{4bc}{3a}$

H. $\dfrac{2b}{15a}$

J. $\dfrac{-bc}{15a}$

K. $\dfrac{-4bc}{9a}$

9. Good Look Textile Company's total revenue in 1998 was 15% less than its total revenue in 1997. If the company's total revenue in 1997 was $20,000, what was its total revenue in 1998?

   A. $ 3,000
   B. $15,000
   C. $17,000
   D. $19,700
   E. $23,000

10. If $x = -|2|$, then $x \cdot |3 - 5| = ?$

    F. −16
    G. −4
    H. 1
    J. 4
    K. 16

11. If 20% of the marbles in a sack are red, 60% are blue, and the remaining 24 are green, how many marbles in the sack are red?

    A. 12
    B. 20
    C. 24
    D. 72
    E. 120

12. What is the difference between the least common multiple and the greatest common factor of 8, 12, and 16?

    F. 12
    G. 36
    H. 44
    J. 46
    K. 48

13. In the standard (x, y) coordinate plane shown below, line ℓ_1 is always parallel to line segment $\overline{AB}$, and it can be moved toward or away from $\overline{AB}$. If the resulting rectangle $ABCD$ is to have a perimeter of 18 units, which of the following should be the coordinates of point C?

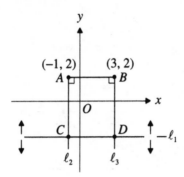

A. $(-1, -3)$
B. $(-3, -1)$
C. $(-1, 3)$
D. $(-1, -5)$
E. $(-1, -6)$

14. Which of the following is equal to $(x - y)[5(x - y) - 3(y - x)]$?

F. $2(x - y)$
G. $2(x - y)^2$
H. $8(x - y)$
J. $8(x - y)^2$
K. $8(x - y)^3$

15. In the figure below, given triangles *ABC* and *AED,* what is the measure of *x*?

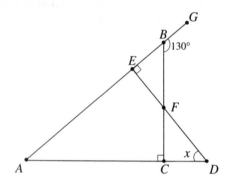

A. 30°
B. 40°
C. 50°
D. 60°
E. 70°

16. A line connects points (3, 4) and (7, 1) in a standard (*x, y*) coordinate plane. What is the slope of this line?

F. $\frac{4}{3}$

G. $\frac{3}{4}$

H. $\frac{3}{7}$

J. $-\frac{3}{4}$

K. $-\frac{4}{3}$

17. A stereo that normally sells for $100 is discounted by 20%. If Sadeka buys the stereo at the discounted price and pays 8% sales tax, how much does she spend on the stereo, including the sales tax?

A. $73.60
B. $82.00
C. $82.80
D. $86.40
E. $88.00

18. In the figure below, the area of $\triangle ABC$ is 20 square inches. What is the length of $\overline{CD}$, in inches?

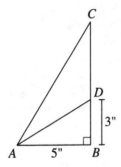

F. 1
G. 2
H. 3
J. 5
K. 8

19. Sean spent 60% of his total earnings on music CDs. He spent 80% of the remaining amount on clothes. If x represents his total earnings, which of the following is the amount he spent on clothes?

   A. $0.14x$
   B. $0.32x$
   C. $0.48x$
   D. $0.52x$
   E. $0.68x$

20. What is the product of the binomials $(p - q^3)(5p - 2q^2)$?

   F. $5p^2 - 2pq^2 - 5pq^3 + 2q^5$
   G. $5p^2 - 2pq^2 - 5pq^3 - 2q^5$
   H. $5p^2 - 2pq^2 + 5pq^3 + 2q^5$
   J. $5p^2 - 7pq^3 + 2q^6$
   K. $5p^2 - 7pq^3 + 2q^5$

21. In a store, 3 pencils and 2 notebooks cost $2.20. If the cost of a notebook is 4 times the cost of a pencil, what is the cost of each pencil?

   A. $0.11
   B. $0.20
   C. $0.22
   D. $0.40
   E. $0.80

22. If there are 1,760 yards in a mile and 1 mile is equal to 1.6 kilometers, how many yards are there in 2 kilometers?

    F.   220

    G. 1,100

    H. 2,200

    J. 2,816

    K. 5,632

23. Jan is exactly 15 years older than Sue. In exactly 5 years, Jan will be twice as old as Sue. What is Sue's current age, in years?

    A. 10

    B. 15

    C. 20

    D. 25

    E. 30

24. The number of bacteria, N, in a container is given by the equation $N = 1 + 1.5t + 25t^2$, where t is the time, in seconds, after the bacteria are first collected. How many bacteria are in the container 10 seconds after the bacteria are first collected?

    F.   265

    G.   516

    H. 2,516

    J. 2,651

    K. 4,001

25. In the figure below, $\overline{BC} = \overline{CD}$. What is the perimeter, in feet, of the figure shown?

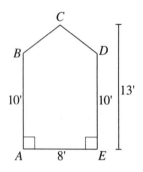

- **A.** 28
- **B.** 31
- **C.** 34
- **D.** 36
- **E.** 38

26. Which of the following most closely corresponds to the position of point P shown in the number line below?

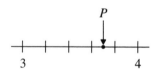

- **F.** 3.07
- **G.** 3.35
- **H.** 3.40
- **J.** 3.70
- **K.** 3.80

27. If x lies between $\frac{1}{3}$ and $\frac{2}{3}$, which of the following could be the value of x?

    A. $\frac{4}{5}$

    B. $\frac{3}{4}$

    C. $\frac{5}{6}$

    D. $\frac{2}{5}$

    E. $\frac{2}{7}$

28. In the figure below, $ABCD$ is a rhombus, and $\overline{AE}$ is a line segment. If $\overline{AB} = 4$ inches, what is the area of the shaded $\triangle CED$, in square inches?

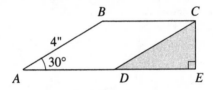

    F. $\sqrt{3}$
    G. $3\sqrt{2}$
    H. $2\sqrt{3}$
    J. $4\sqrt{2}$
    K. $4\sqrt{3}$

29. In a sack, there are R red marbles and G green marbles. If N people are each given 3 red marbles and 5 green marbles from the sack, 2 red marbles and 2 green marbles remain in the sack. Which of the following could be the values of R, G, and N?

A. $R = 16, G = 16, N = 5$
B. $R = 20, G = 33, N = 6$
C. $R = 17, G = 28, N = 5$
D. $R = 32, G = 52, N = 10$
E. $R = 22, G = 37, N = 7$

30. What is the greatest surface area, in square units, that can be covered by a triangle whose three sides are 9, 12, and 15 units long?

F. 54
G. 67.5
H. 90
J. 108
K. 135

31. If $y_1 = 5x - 3$ and $y_2 = 2x + 6$ represent two lines in a standard (x, y) coordinate plane, which of the following represents the coordinates of the point at which the lines intersect each other?

A. $(0, -3)$
B. $(0, 6)$
C. $(1, 2)$
D. $(1, 8)$
E. $(3, 12)$

32. In a standard (x, y) coordinate plane, what is the area, in square units, of the triangle enclosed by the x-axis, the y-axis, and the line whose equation is $3y = -4x + 12$?

   F.   5

   G.   6

   H.   10

   J.   12

   K.   25

33. Rectangle A and rectangle B have equal areas. If the ratio of the length of rectangle A to the width of rectangle B is $2 : 1$, then the ratio of the width of rectangle A to the length of rectangle B is which of the following?

   A. $2 : 1$

   B. $1 : 2$

   C. $4 : 1$

   D. $4 : 2$

   E. $1 : 4$

34. Car P travels at p miles per hour, and car Q travels at q miles per hour. Which of the following represents the combined distance traveled by car P and car Q in h hours?

   F. $\dfrac{p+q}{h}$

   G. $h^2(p+q)$

   H. $h(pq)$

   J. $h^2(pq)$

   K. $h(p+q)$

35. Which of the following is the graph of the solution set of
$2x < 4x - 8$?

A.

B.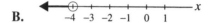

C. ⊦—+—+—+—⊕—▶ x
   0 1 2 3 4

D. ⊦—+—◀—⊕—— x
   0 1 2 3 4

E. ⊦—+—+—●—▶ x
   0 1 2 3 4

36. Gino scored 50 on the first test, 70 on the second test, and 90 on the third test. If the first two tests count 30% each and the third test counts 40% of the overall average, what is Gino's overall average?

F. 62
G. 70
H. 72
J. 75
K. 82

37. Which of the following is the best approximation of the perimeter, in inches, of the triangle shown below?

(Note: You may use the following values, which are correct to two decimal places:

$\sin 50° = .77$, $\cos 50° = .64$, $\tan 50° = 1.19$)

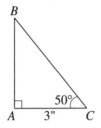

A. 4.7
B. 7.3
C. 8.3
D. 11.5
E. 12.0

38. In the equation

$$x = \frac{60}{p}$$

p is a prime number and x is an integer. What is the smallest possible value of x?

F. 10
G. 12
H. 15
J. 30
K. 60

39. In the figure below, points *A, B,* and *C* are on the same line. If
$2x = y$, what is the measure of *x*?

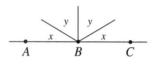

A. 15°
B. 30°
C. 40°
D. 45°
E. 60°

40. A line in a standard (*x, y*) coordinate plane touches the *y*-axis 4
units above the *x*-axis. Which of the following could be the
equation of that line?

F. $y = 4x$
G. $4y = x$
H. $4x + y = 0$
J. $4y + x = 0$
K. $y = x + 4$

41. The figure below shows four equilateral triangles, each of perimeter 3 units. What is the perimeter of the large triangle, △*ABC*?

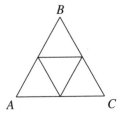

A. 6
B. 9
C. 12
D. 15
E. 18

42. Which of the following could be the values of *x* and *y* in the figure below?

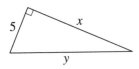

F. $x = 3, y = 4$
G. $x = 4, y = 3$
H. $x = 10, y = 15$
J. $x = 12, y = 13$
K. $x = 13, y = 12$

43. The circumference of a circular patio is 20π feet. What is the area covered by this patio, in square feet?

   A. 10π

   B. 20π

   C.   100

   D. 100π

   E. 400π

44. If $A = \begin{bmatrix} 4 & -1 \\ 3 & 1 \end{bmatrix}$ and $B = \begin{bmatrix} 5 & -1 \\ -4 & 2 \end{bmatrix}$, then $A - B = ?$

   F. $\begin{bmatrix} 9 & -2 \\ -1 & 3 \end{bmatrix}$

   G. $\begin{bmatrix} -1 & -2 \\ 7 & 3 \end{bmatrix}$

   H. $\begin{bmatrix} 9 & 0 \\ -1 & -1 \end{bmatrix}$

   J. $\begin{bmatrix} -1 & 0 \\ 7 & -1 \end{bmatrix}$

   K. $\begin{bmatrix} 20 & 1 \\ -12 & 2 \end{bmatrix}$

45. The perimeter of a rectangle is 22 inches. If the width of the rectangle is 4 inches, what is the area, in square inches, of the largest triangle enclosed by the rectangle?

A. 14
B. 28
C. 44
D. 56
E. 60

46. In the figure below, *AB* is a line that passes through the origin of a standard (*x, y*) coordinate plane. The coordinates of point *P* are (*x, 3x*). Which of the following points lies outside (that is, to the right of) the shaded region?

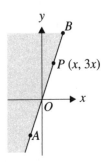

F. (−1, −1)
G. (1, 1)
H. (−2, −3)
J. (−2, −4)
K. (3, 10)

47. In the figure shown below, $\triangle ABE$ and $\triangle ACD$ are two right triangles, $\overline{BE} = 3$ feet, $\overline{BC} = x$ feet, and $\overline{CD} = x$ feet. Which of the following is the closest approximation of x, in feet?

(Note: You may use the following values.

$\sin 20° = \frac{17}{50}$, $\cos 20° = \frac{47}{50}$, and $\tan 20° = \frac{9}{25}$)

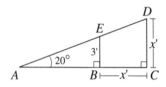

A. 2.2
B. 4.8
C. 5.0
D. 5.5
E. 6.0

48. $\log_2(\log_2 2 + \log_2 2) = ?$

F. 1
G. $2(\log_2 2)$
H. $3(\log_2 2)$
J. $\log_2(2^3)$
K. $2[\log_2(2^2)]$

49. For all people taller than 5 feet, a medical guide makes recommendations about how much a person should weigh, given that person's height. The recommendation is given by

$$\text{weight} = 2.2\,(\text{height}) + 6$$

where weight is measured in pounds and height in inches.

Raul is 65 inches tall and weighs 160 pounds. According to the formula above, Raul:

A. is 11 pounds over the recommended weight.
B. is 11 pounds under the recommended weight.
C. weighs the same as the recommended weight.
D. is 21 pounds over the recommended weight.
E. is 21 pounds under the recommended weight.

50. In the figure below, O is the center of a semicircle of radius 2 units. What is the area of $\triangle OAB$, in square units?

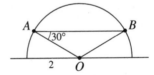

F. $\sqrt{3}$
G. 2
H. $2\sqrt{3}$
J. 4
K. $3\sqrt{2}$

51. When a stone is tossed into a lake, ripples are generated. If the radius of the circular area enclosed by a ripple doubles every second, and the radius of the circular area enclosed by a ripple 2 seconds after a stone is tossed is 5 feet, what is the area, in square feet, enclosed by the same ripple, 5 seconds after the stone is tossed?

A. 80π
B. 400π
C. 900π
D. $1,600\pi$
E. $3,200\pi$

52. To get to school, 30% of the students ride their bikes and the rest take the bus. If 40% of the students are boys and 60% are girls, which of the following represents the probability that any student chosen at random from the school will be a girl who rides her bike to school?

F. 0.12
G. 0.18
H. 0.28
J. 0.42
K. 0.62

53. The total cost of manufacturing a pencil consists of the cost of the wood and the cost of the lead. For each pencil, the cost of the lead is twice the cost of the wood. If the cost of manufacturing 250 pencils is t dollars and the cost of the lead for each pencil is p cents, what is the relationship between t and p? (Assume that no other costs are involved.)

A. $t = \dfrac{3p}{5}$

B. $t = \dfrac{15p}{4}$

C. $t = \dfrac{15p}{2}$

D. $t = 375p$

E. $t = 750p$

54. In the figure below, $\triangle BAC$ is a right triangle with base 10 inches and height 5 inches. If $\overline{AD} = x$ and $\overline{AD}$ is perpendicular to $\overline{BC}$, what is the value of x, in inches?

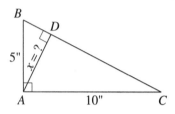

F. 4

G. $2\sqrt{5}$

H. $\dfrac{10}{\sqrt{3}}$

J. $5\sqrt{5}$

K. Cannot be determined from the given information

55. If a fair coin is tossed 4 times, what is the probability of tossing a head, a head, a tail, and a head in exactly that order?

(Note: A fair coin is one for which the outcome of heads and the outcome of tails are equally likely.)

A. $\frac{1}{16}$

B. $\frac{1}{8}$

C. $\frac{3}{16}$

D. $\frac{1}{4}$

E. $\frac{3}{4}$

56. In a class of five students, the average score on a quiz is 6, the median score is 5, and the highest score is 15. If all five students receive different scores and all scores are positive integers, what is the *greatest* possible value of the second highest score?

F. 6
G. 7
H. 8
J. 9
K. 10

57. If $3x + y = 15$, then $4.5x + 1.5y = ?$

A. 16.50
B. 21.50
C. 22.50
D. 33.75
E. Cannot be determined from the given information

58. Given the equation of an ellipse as

$$\frac{(x+4)^2}{9} + \frac{(y-2)^2}{16} = 1$$

which of the following would be the coordinates of the center of the ellipse in the standard (x, y) coordinate plane?

F. $(3, 4)$
G. $(4, -2)$
H. $(-4, 2)$
J. $(-3, -4)$
K. $(2, -4)$

59. A storage room in the shape of a rectangular box is 12 feet high, and the dimensions of its floor are 4 feet by 3 feet. What is the length (in feet) of the longest stick that can fit in this room?

  A. $\sqrt{119}$
  B. 13
  C. 15
  D. 17
  E. $\sqrt{381}$

60. The password for a computer account has to contain 8 characters. Each character must be a letter of the alphabet, a number from 0 to 9 inclusive, the pound sign (#), or the dollar sign ($). Upper-case letters of the alphabet are considered different from lower-case letters. Which of the following represents the maximum number of different passwords possible given these rules?

  F. $2^5(3^2)$
  G. 2^9
  H. 2^{14}
  J. 2^{16}
  K. 2^{48}

STOP. IF YOU FINISH BEFORE TIME IS UP, CHECK YOUR WORK ON THIS SECTION ONLY. DO NOT WORK ON ANY OTHER SECTION IN THE TEST.

Time: 35 Minutes
40 Questions

Each of the four passages in this test is followed by questions. Read the passage and choose the best answer to each question. Return to the passage as often as necessary to answer the questions.

PASSAGE I

Prose fiction: This passage is from the opening of *Sister Carrie,* a novel by Theodore Dreiser published in 1900.

When Caroline Meeber boarded the afternoon train for Chicago, her total outfit consisted of a small trunk, a cheap imitation alligator-skin satchel, a small lunch in a paper box, and a yellow leather snap purse, containing her ticket, a scrap
5 of paper with her sister's address in Van Buren Street, and four dollars in money. It was in August, 1889. She was eighteen years of age, bright, timid, and full of the illusions of ignorance and youth. Whatever touch of regret at parting characterized her thoughts, it was certainly not for advantages now
10 being given up. A gush of tears at her mother's farewell kiss, a touch in her throat when the cars clacked by the flour mill where her father worked by the day, a pathetic sign as the familiar green environs of the village passed in review, and the threads which bound her so lightly to girlhood and home
15 were irretrievably broken.

To be sure there was always the next station, where one might descend and return. There was the great city, bound more closely by these very trains which came up daily. Columbia City was not so very far away, even once she was
20 in Chicago. What, pray, is a few hours—a few hundred miles?

She looked at the little slip bearing her sister's address and wondered. She gazed at the green landscape, now passing in swift review, until her swifter thoughts replaced its impression with vague conjectures of what Chicago might be.

25   When a girl leaves her home at eighteen, she does one of two things. Either she falls into saving hands and becomes better, or she rapidly assumes the cosmopolitan standard of virtue and becomes worse. Of an intermediate balance, under the circumstances, there is no possibility. The city has its cunning

30   wiles, no less than the infinitely smaller and more human tempter. There are large forces which allure with all the soulfulness of expression possible in the most cultured human. The gleam of a thousand lights is often as effective as the persuasive light in a wooing and fascinating eye. Half the undo-

35   ing of the unsophisticated and natural mind is accomplished by forces wholly superhuman. A blare of sound, a roar of life, a vast array of human hives, appeal to the astonished senses in equivocal terms. Without a counselor at hand to whisper cautious interpretations, what falsehoods may not these things

40   breathe into the unguarded ear! Unrecognized for what they are, their beauty, like music, too often relaxes, then weakens, then perverts the simpler human perceptions.

Caroline, or Sister Carrie, as she had been half affectionately termed by the family, was possessed of a mind rudimentary in

45   its power of observation and analysis. Self-interest with her was high, but not strong. It was, nevertheless, her guiding characteristic. Warm with the fancies of youth, pretty with the insipid prettiness of the formative period, possessed of a figure promising eventual shapeliness and an eye alight with cer-

50   tain native intelligence, she was a fair example of the middle American class—two generations removed from the emigrant. Books were beyond her interest—knowledge a sealed book. In the intuitive graces she was still crude. She could scarcely toss her head gracefully. Her hands were almost inef-

55   fectual. The feet, though small, were set flatly. And yet she

was interested in her charms, quick to understand the keener pleasures of life, ambitious to gain in material things. A half-equipped little knight she was, venturing to reconnoiter the mysterious city and dreaming wild dreams of some vague, far-

60   off supremacy, which should make it prey and subject—the proper penitent, groveling at a woman's slipper.

"That," said a voice in her ear, "is one of the prettiest little resorts in Wisconsin."

"Is it?" she answered nervously.

65   The train was just pulling out of Waukesha. For some time she had been conscious of a man behind. She felt him observing her mass of hair. He had been fidgeting, and with natural intuition she felt a certain interest growing in that quarter. Her maidenly reserve, and a certain sense of what was conven-

70   tional under the circumstances, called her to forestall and deny this familiarity, but the daring and magnetism of the individual, born of past experiences and triumphs, prevailed. She answered.

He leaned forward to put his elbows upon the back of her

75   seat and proceeded to make himself volubly agreeable.

"Yes, that is a great resort for Chicago people. The hotels are swell. You are not familiar with this part of the country, are you?"

"Oh, yes, I am," answered Carrie. "That is, I live at

80   Columbia City. I have never been through here though."

"And so this is your first visit to Chicago," he observed.

All the time she was conscious of certain features out of the side of her eye. Flush, colorful cheeks, a light mustache, a gray fedora hat. She now turned and looked upon him in full, the

85   instincts of self-protection and coquetry mingling confusedly in her brain.

"I didn't say that," she said.

"Oh," he answered, in a very pleasing way and with an assumed air of mistake, "I thought you did."

1. From the passage, it is reasonable to infer that Caroline Meeber comes from a:

   A. poor immigrant family.
   B. poor but socially ambitious midwestern family.
   C. hard-working but uncaring family.
   D. fairly typical middle-class midwestern family.

2. Lines 16–20 indicate Carrie's:

   F. naiveté.
   G. nervousness.
   H. ignorance.
   J. sadness.

3. Which of the following best describes the third paragraph (lines 25–42)?

   A. An interruption by the author that generalizes and comments on Carrie's situation
   B. An angry diatribe against the foolishness of young girls and the dangers of the city
   C. An ironic picture of the typical small-town prejudices against the evils of the city
   D. The author's thoughtful comment on the contrast between small-town and city life

4. In the third paragraph (lines 25–42), the city is compared to:

   F. a seducer.
   G. a web of falsehoods.
   H. a cruel teacher.
   J. a jungle.

5. Which of the following best describes Carrie?

    I.   Unintelligent and unimaginative

   II.   Beautiful and strong-willed

  III.   Unschooled and unsophisticated

    A. I only

    B. II only

    C. II and III only

    D. III only

6. To whom does "the proper penitent, groveling at a woman's slipper" (lines 60–61) refer?

    F. The man on the train

    G. Men in general

    H. Life

    J. Chicago

7. Which of the following does Carrie's exchange with the man on the train indicate about her?

    A. She is open and easy-going.

    B. In spite of her youth, she is experienced in dealing with men.

    C. She is willing to disregard convention when tempted.

    D. She longs for wealth and position.

8. The man answers Carrie with "an assumed air of mistake" (lines 88–89) because he:

    F. is embarrassed about his mistake.

    G. has been lying to her.

    H. wants to ingratiate himself with her.

    J. is poking fun at her.

9. From evidence in this passage only, it is reasonable to assume that in Chicago Carrie will be a:

    A. strong, ambitious manipulator.

    B. victim of the city and of her own character.

    C. positive influence on everyone she meets.

    D. tragic heroine.

10. Which of the following best describes the author's view of Sister Carrie?

    F. Detached

    G. Affectionate

    H. Disgusted

    J. Ironic

PASSAGE II

Social science: This passage is from *The Family in the Western World from the Black Death to the Industrial Age* by Beatrice Gottlieb (© 1993 by Oxford University Press).

    The links between generations are forged by inheritance. Apart from biological matter, which even plants inherit, all manner of things can be inherited by human beings. Laws and customs determine what they are. Some inheritance takes
5   place at birth and remains throughout a person's life. Things inherited in this way are usually intangible. Other inheritance takes place later, often when an older person dies and passes a (usually) tangible resource on to someone younger.

    Inheritance provides one of the contrasts between our time
10 and the centuries before industrialization. What used to be a pervasive principle has become limited, and what was a public concern has become a private one. It is still common for people to inherit property, and there are laws that protect the rights of heirs, but modern Western society does not entirely
15 approve of inherited wealth, and it is not considered necessary to inherit something in order to get on in the world. Inherited

wealth is regarded with some suspicion and is heavily taxed.
By contrast, in the past *everything* tended to be inherited.

20 There were three main categories of things that were inherited: material, social, and personal. Material legacies are real property and other wealth. In the past, although land was bought and sold, its normal route from one person to another was by inheritance. This alone explains why inheritance loomed so large in people's lives. Not only outright ownership

25 of land but also the mere right to use it could be inherited, and it was often this right, rather than ownership, that peasants passed along to their heirs. Wealth of any kind, even if it was acquired by purchase or as a gift, tended to become hereditary sooner or later.

30 Social legacies included name, status, and occupation. What is today only sometimes inherited used to be always inherited, and what is now given to heirs by choice used to be the heirs' legal right. Only surnames now have the legal standing that all these social assets used to have. At the highest levels of

35 society, titles as well as names were inherited. An indication of how things have changed is the fact that, in modern Britain, most new titles conferred by the state, such as knighthoods and life peerages, are not hereditary, while in the past, much of their value lay in the very fact that they were hereditary.

40 Status in the past was enshrined in the law and regarded as hereditary and fixed. A slave, a serf, a bourgeois, a gentleman, a lady, or a noble was usually what he or she was from birth. Although nobody was born a clergyman, many churchmen very nearly inherited their clerical status because they held

45 positions that were virtually hereditary, like a whole gamut of other inherited occupations, jobs, and offices. Peasants who held village "offices" usually inherited them, from mayor and reeve to shepherd and woodward. Even the man whose job in one French town was transporting infants to wet nurses was

50 likely to be the son of the previous holder of the job. In eighteenth-century France, at the same time that nobles of ancient family were claiming their exclusive right to certain high

offices, shepherds in the countryside were insisting, sometimes in violent demonstrations, that their jobs were strictly
55 hereditary.

Personal assets include physical traits and intangibles like
character and health. In the past there was a tendency to min-
imize environment and upbringing and put all the emphasis
on inheritance. To be granted the status of burgher in many a
60 European town, a man had to offer proof of "good birth" and
the absence of disease in both his parents, specifically the
dreaded disease of leprosy. A nobleman in theory was not
merely someone who was lucky enough to have parents who
filled a certain social niche at the time of his birth but some-
65 one who actually inherited nobility, a quality of character that
resided in the blood. Slaves were servile and peasants were
boorish because it was in their blood to be so. Deeply
entrenched notions about the connection of class and character and the inheritability of both propped up the hierarchical
70 structure of society and persisted into later, supposedly more
democratic, times as ingredients of racism.

11. It can reasonably be inferred from the first paragraph of the passage (lines 1–8) that:

A. a person's legal inheritance in tenth-century England would
be different from his or her legal inheritance in twentieth-
century England.

B. intangible qualities such as artistic talent have always been
considered a more valuable inheritance than money or
property.

C. the term *inheritance* should not be used to describe the trans-
fer of biological matter from one generation to the next.

D. inheritance of your father's surname is tangible, whereas the
inheritance of his property is intangible.

12. The second paragraph of the passage implies that one of the reasons inherited wealth is heavily taxed today is that:

   F. the lower and middle classes would revolt otherwise.
   G. wealthy people are thought to be noble and therefore happy to help the less fortunate through taxes.
   H. it is easier to tax people who have inherited their wealth than it is to tax people who have earned theirs.
   J. there is a belief that people are less entitled to inherited wealth than to money they themselves earn.

13. Based on the passage, which of the following best contrasts the concept of inheritance in the past with the concept of inheritance in the twentieth century?

   A. In the past, the inheritance of physical traits was not considered important, whereas today it is.
   B. Inheritance was always a matter of law in the past, whereas today it is always a matter of custom.
   C. The right to use land was often inherited in the past, whereas it is infrequent today.
   D. Inheritance is a less public and legal concern in the Western world today than it was in earlier centuries.

14. According to the passage, material inheritance was more important in the past because:

   F. it was the usual way that land was passed on.
   G. it wasn't possible to purchase land, as it is today.
   H. land was scarce and only wealthy families could own it.
   J. inherited land was not taxed as heavily as purchased land.

15. According to the passage, which of the following would be classified as social inheritance?

   A. A person's right to use land his or her father had used
   B. Knighthood
   C. Nobility of character
   D. A country manor

16. According to the passage, which of the following is still inherited as a matter of law?

    F. A surname
    G. Money
    H. A high position in the church
    J. Personal property

17. The example of the job of transporting infants to wet nurses (lines 48–50) is used by the author to:

    A. illustrate the absurdity of legal inheritance.
    B. illustrate material inheritance.
    C. show that even minor occupations often went from father to son.
    D. contrast the customs of inheritance in France with those in England.

18. Based on the passage, which of the following is a reasonable conclusion about the attitude toward heredity in previous centuries?

    F. Heredity and environment were seen as equal.
    G. Heredity was seen as the basis of character, with environment playing little or no role.
    H. Environment was considered the chief factor in the development of character traits, whereas heredity was seen as the basis of a person's general health.
    J. Environment was seen the basis of character, with heredity playing little or no role.

19. As it is used in line 69, *hierarchical* most nearly means:

    A. arranged in class or rank order.
    B. rigidly archaic.
    C. arranged according to the organization of the church.
    D. totalitarian.

20. According to the author, modern racism may be related to:

   F. limited education and opportunity for slaves and peasants.

   G. the past custom of hereditary occupations.

   H. a belief that character and class are linked and are hereditary.

   J. genes that predispose people to be boorish and intolerant.

PASSAGE III

Humanities: This passage is from a study of the Renaissance painter Leonardo da Vinci: *The World of Leonardo* by Robert Wallace and the editors of Time-Life Books (© 1966 by Time Inc.).

Leonardo contributed much of the landscape for the *Baptism.* It is not in Verrocchio's style—its pools and mists, patches of sunlight and shadow, prefigure the magical and almost hallucinatory landscape of the *Mona Lisa.* The land-
5 scape and the angel are done in oil, a medium that had only lately been introduced to Italy from the north, while Verrocchio's parts of the picture are in the traditional egg tempera. The latter ensured a bright enamel-like surface, but demanded strict demarcation between one color and another.
10 It was entirely in character for the young Leonardo, who was to become the most avant-garde and experimental painter of his time, to seize on oil while his master continued in the old way.

One of the chief advantages of oil was the possibility of
15 nuances of effect, and Leonardo began to explore these in the background of the *Baptism.* There he uses aerial perspective, which is quite different from the mathematical, linear perspective of Brunelleschi. By dictionary definition, aerial perspective is the creation of depth in painting by the use of
20 gradations in color and directness; to Leonardo it was much more than that. He thought of air, atmosphere, as an almost palpable mass of particles floating between the eye and the objects it perceives—a transparent ocean in which all things exist and by which they are bound together. Air, full of light
25 and humidity, haze and shadow, has a unifying function that

brings foreground and background into relationship. Leonardo devoted years of his life and scores of pages of manuscript to studies of atmosphere and how to create the illusion of it in painting. His use of oil glazes to produce aerial per-
30 spective does not appear as very impressive in the dirty, overpainted, and varnish-clouded background of the *Baptism,* but it is there, revealing his concern with it even at the beginning of his career.

Thus from the outset Leonardo regarded landscape not sim-
35 ply as a backdrop for studies of the human figure. He saw man in his whole environment, as an inextricable part of nature. Many years later, when he brought his early ideas to written form in his notes for his *Treatise on Painting,* he took to task no less a painter than Sandro Botticelli, who did not share his
40 feeling for landscape. (It was extraordinary for Leonardo to reproach another artist by name. He avoided quarrels, and when he was abused by his young rival, Michelangelo, who hated him, he made no reply other than to note in his journal that it is wise to cultivate patience.) "He is not well rounded,"
45 wrote Leonardo, "who does not have an equally keen interest in all of the things within the compass of painting; for example, if someone does not delight in landscape, he therefore considers this to be a matter requiring only brief and rudimentary study. Thus, our Botticelli has declared this particular
50 study to be vain, for if one but threw a sponge full of colors at the wall, it would leave a patch in which one might see a beautiful landscape. It is probably true that one may see all sorts of things in such a patch—that is, if one wishes to look for them—such as human heads, different kinds of animals, bat-
55 tles, cliffs, the sea, clouds of forests, and other such things; it is just like the sound of bells in which you can imagine hearing whatever words you please. But even though such patches may help you to invent things, they will never teach you how to carry any particular project to completion. And that painter
60 painted very sorry landscapes."

The point of Leonardo's swipe at Botticelli is plain enough: landscape is no trivial thing. But it is worth noting that he does not entirely dismiss the idea of studying a random, colored patch for the images which might appear in it. In another part
65 of his *Treatise* he actually recommends staring at stains on walls as a source of inspiration; the nineteenth-century French author-painter Victor Hugo, following Leonardo, derived many of his ideas for drawings from the blots made by coffee stains on tablecloths.

21. According to the first paragraph (lines 1–14), one of the reasons Leonardo's work on the *Baptism* is different from Verrocchio's is that:

    A. it is better.

    B. Leonardo's colors are bright and enamel-like.

    C. Leonardo worked in oil.

    D. it disregards perspective.

22. From the first paragraph (lines 1–14), the reader learns that:

    F. Verrocchio was Leonardo's master.

    G. Leonardo and Verrocchio were competitors.

    H. Leonardo idolized Verrocchio.

    J. Verrocchio disapproved of Leonardo's avant-garde techniques.

23. According to the passage, aerial perspective:

    A. is more realistic than linear perspective.

    B. uses gradations of colors to create a sense of depth in a painting.

    C. is perspective from above rather than in front of a painting.

    D. was first used by Brunelleschi and later improved upon by Leonardo.

24. Which of the following best describes Leonardo's approach to perspective in a painting?

    F. His lines converge on a central vanishing point.

    G. He combines egg tempera and oil to soften the lines of objects.

    H. He creates the illusion of air, or atmosphere, bringing foreground and background into relationship.

    J. Objects in the foreground are created in brighter colors and are larger than objects in the background.

25. Leonardo's contribution to the *Baptism* is primarily significant because:

    A. his use of oil glazes shows his mastery of the medium.

    B. he later used the same background in the *Mona Lisa.*

    C. it shows his early recognition of the importance of atmosphere.

    D. it is proof that even early in his career he proved himself superior to his contemporaries.

26. According to the passage, which of the following best describes Leonardo's relationship with Michelangelo?

    F. Leonardo thought that Michelangelo wasn't a well-rounded painter and criticized him in the *Treatise on Painting.*

    G. Michelangelo hated Leonardo and didn't hide his feelings, but Leonardo didn't respond.

    H. Michelangelo disagreed with Leonardo's theories, and Leonardo disliked Michelangelo's landscapes.

    J. Leonardo and Michelangelo quarreled constantly about principles of painting.

27. Leonardo found fault with Botticelli because that artist:

    A. refused to use aerial perspective in his paintings.

    B. was a careless, haphazard painter.

    C. created his works by throwing a sponge full of colors at the canvas.

    D. didn't believe it was important to study landscapes.

28. It is reasonable to infer from the passage that Leonardo:

    F. was at odds with most other painters during this period because of his radical ideas.

    G. was interested in creating paintings but cared nothing for theories or the works of other artists.

    H. believed that the painters who came before him were more skillful than his contemporaries.

    J. was interested in the works of other artists but liked to experiment with new techniques in his own works.

29. *Dirty,* as it is used in line 30, most nearly means:

    A. dark, clouded.

    B. vulgar.

    C. soiled.

    D. unpleasant, ugly.

30. Which of the following best describes the last paragraph of the passage (lines 61–69)?

    F. It moves away from the subject of the importance of landscapes.

    G. It supports Botticelli's attitude toward the unimportance of landscapes.

    H. It summarizes the previous three paragraphs.

    J. It compares the works of Leonardo and the nineteenth-century author-painter Victor Hugo.

PASSAGE IV

Natural science: This passage is from Daniel Sperlings's "The Case for Electric Vehicles" (*Scientific American,* November 1996).

Cars account for half the oil consumed in the U.S., about half the urban pollution and one-fourth the greenhouse gases. They take a similar toll of resources in other industrial nations and in the cities of the developing world. As vehicle use continues
5   to increase in the coming decade, the U.S. and other countries will have to addreess these issues or else face unacceptable economic, health-related and political costs. It is unlikely that oil prices will remain at their current low level or that other nations will accept a large and growing U.S. contribution to
10 global climatic change.

Policymakers and industry have four options: reduce vehicle use, increase the efficiency and reduce the emissions of conventional gasoline-powered vehicles, switch to less noxious fuels, or find less polluting propulsion systems. The last
15 of these—in particular the introduction of vehicles powered by electricity—is ultimately the only sustainable option. The other alternatives are attractive in theory but in practice are either impractical or offer only marginal improvements. For example, reduced vehicle use could solve congestion woes
20 and a host of social and environmental problems, but evidence from around the world suggests that it is very difficult to make people give up their cars to any significant extent. In the U.S., mass-transit ridership and carpooling have declined since World War II. Even in western Europe, with fuel prices aver-
25 aging more than $1 a liter (about $4 a gallon) and with pervasive mass transit and dense populations, cars still account for 80 percent of all passenger travel.

Improved energy efficiency is also appealing, but automotive fuel economy has barely budged in 10 years. Alternative
30 fuels such as methanol or natural gas, burned in internal-combustion engines, could be introduced at relatively low cost, but

they would lead to only marginal reductions in pollution and greenhouse emissions (especially because oil companies are already spending billions of dollars every year to develop less

35 polluting formulations of gasoline).

Electric-drive vehicles (those whose wheels are turned by electric motors rather than by a mechanical gasoline-powered drivetrain) could reduce urban pollution and greenhouse emissions significantly over the coming decade. And they could

40 lay a foundation for a transportation system that would ultimately be almost pollution-free. Although electrically driven vehicles have a history as old as that of the internal-combustion engine, a number of recent technological developments—including by-products of both the computer

45 revolution and the Strategic Defense Initiative (SDI) in the 1980s—promise to make this form of transportation efficient and inexpensive enough to compete with gasoline. Overcoming the entrenched advantages of gas-powered cars, however, will require a concerted effort on the parts of indus-

50 try and government to make sure that the environmental benefits accruing from electric cars return to consumers as concrete incentives for purchase.

The term "electric-drive vehicle" includes not only those cars powered by batteries charged with household current but

55 also vehicles that generate electricity onboard or store it in devices other than batteries. Their common denominator is an efficient electric motor that drives the wheels and extracts energy from the car's motion when it slows down. Internal combustion vehicles, in contrast, employ a constantly running

60 engine whose power is diverted through a series of gears and clutches to drive the wheels and to turn a generator for the various electrically powered accessories in the car.

Electric vehicles are more efficient—and thus generally less polluting—than internal-combustion vehicles for a variety of

65 reasons. First, because the electric motor is directly connected to the wheels, it consumes no energy while the car is at rest or

coasting, increasing the effective efficiency by roughly one fifth. Regenerative braking schemes—which employ the motor as a generator when the car is slowing down—can
70 return as much as half an electric vehicle's kinetic energy to the storage cells, giving it a major advantage in stop-and-go urban traffic.

Furthermore, the motor converts more than 90 percent of the energy in its storage cells to motive forces, whereas internal-
75 combustion drives utilize less than 25 percent of the energy in a liter of gasoline. Although the storage cells are typically charged by an electricity generating system, the efficiency of which averages only 33 percent, an electric drive still has a significant 5 percent net advantage over internal combustion.
80 Innovations such as combined-cycle generation (which extracts additional energy from the exhaust heat of a conventional power plant) will soon make it possible for the utility power plants from which the storage cells are charged to raise their efficiency to as much as 50 percent. This boost would
85 increase proportionately the fraction of energy ultimately delivered to the wheels of an electric vehicle. Fuel cells, which "burn" hydrogen to generate electricity directly onboard an electric car, are even more efficient.

31. What is the main function of the first paragraph (lines 1–10) of the passage?

    A. To criticize recent developments in automobile efficiency

    B. To show the relationship between cars and global warming

    C. To summarize some of the main problems created by internal-combustion cars

    D. To indicate the attitudes of other nations toward the U.S. contribution to climatic change

32. In paragraph two (lines 11–27), the author cites the high fuel prices in western Europe to:

    F. compare them to prices in the U.S., which are much lower.
    G. show that even high fuel prices don't significantly reduce the number of drivers.
    H. account for the greater use of mass transit in Europe than in the United States.
    J. advocate vehicles powered by electricity rather than by fossil fuels.

33. According to the passage, methanol as a fuel would NOT be the best solution to problems caused by gasoline because:

    A. it wouldn't significantly reduce pollution.
    B. the cost of introducing it is prohibitively high.
    C. it is inadequate as a fuel for high-powered vehicles.
    D. oil companies would spend billions of dollars lobbying against it.

34. It is reasonable to assume from the passage that the author would agree with which of the following statements?

    F. Electric cars are superior to gas-powered cars in every way.
    G. As they become less expensive, electric cars will compete more effectively with cars that use gasoline.
    H. For the sake of a clean environment, consumers will easily give up gas-powered cars for electric ones.
    J. The only reason that electric vehicles have not been accepted by more people is that they cost too much.

35. Why does the author of the passage reject reduced vehicle use as a solution to the problems caused by cars?

    A. Reduced vehicle use would cause a drastic reduction in fuel prices, hurting the world economy.

    B. It is an unrealistic solution because people will simply not stop using their cars.

    C. Developing countries need to increase—not reduce—their use of vehicles if they intend to keep up with industrial countries.

    D. Even with reduced vehicle use, improvement of the atmosphere would be marginal.

36. One important difference between an electric-drive vehicle and an internal-combustion vehicle is:

    F. an electrical-drive vehicle doesn't rely on a constantly running engine for its power.

    G. an electrical-drive vehicle is more efficient but less powerful than an internal-combustion vehicle.

    H. electrically driven vehicles do not employ regenerative braking schemes as internal-combustion vehicles do.

    J. electrically driven vehicles use alternative fuels that cause less pollution than gasoline.

37. As it is used in line 74, the word *motive* most nearly means:

    A. automotive.

    B. intentional.

    C. causing power.

    D. causing motion.

38. According to the passage, an electric motor's net efficiency advantage over an internal-combustion engine is:

    F. 90 percent.

    G. 65 percent.

    H. 25 percent.

    J. 5 percent.

39. Combined-cycle generation will help improve the efficiency of electric vehicles by:

   A. increasing the efficiency of power plants that charge their storage cells.
   B. decreasing the energy required for an electric car during rest or coasting.
   C. increasing the amount of energy in storage cells by "burning" hydrogen.
   D. extracting energy from a car's exhaust heat.

40. It is reasonable to assume from the passage that:

   F. electric-drive vehicles will inevitably replace internal-combustion vehicles.
   G. the use of carpooling and mass transit will continue to increase in the future.
   H. new technology in other fields may lead to improvements in electric cars.
   J. oil companies will develop methanol and natural gas as alternatives to fossil fuels.

STOP. IF YOU FINISH BEFORE TIME IS UP, CHECK YOUR WORK ON THIS SECTION ONLY. DO NOT WORK ON ANY OTHER SECTION IN THE TEST.

Time: 35 Minutes
40 Questions

DIRECTIONS

Each of the seven passages in this test is followed by several questions. After you read each passage, select the correct choice for each of the questions that follow the passage. Refer to the passage as often as necessary to answer the questions. You may NOT use a calculator on this test.

PASSAGE I

A *fractional distillation column,* shown in Figure 1, separates different size hydrocarbons by a process called refining. Crude oil is heated from a furnace, and as it boils, the vapors move up the distillation column. The vapors cool as they rise and condense at different places in the column according to their boiling points. Figure 2 shows the boiling points of the substances listed in Figure 1. Table 1 gives examples of some uses of these substances.

A Fractional Distillation Column

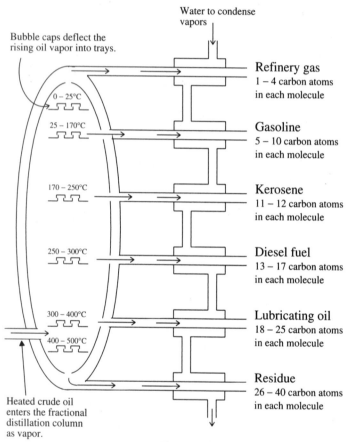

Water to condense vapors

Bubble caps deflect the rising oil vapor into trays.

0 – 25°C

25 – 170°C

170 – 250°C

250 – 300°C

300 – 400°C

400 – 500°C

Refinery gas
1 – 4 carbon atoms in each molecule

Gasoline
5 – 10 carbon atoms in each molecule

Kerosene
11 – 12 carbon atoms in each molecule

Diesel fuel
13 – 17 carbon atoms in each molecule

Lubricating oil
18 – 25 carbon atoms in each molecule

Residue
26 – 40 carbon atoms in each molecule

Heated crude oil enters the fractional distillation column as vapor.

Figure 1

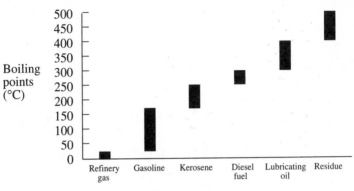

Figure 2

Table 1	
Fractions	Some uses
Refinery gas	fuels and solvents
Gasoline	auto fuel and chemicals
Kerosene	home fuels, plane fuels
Diesel fuel	diesel engines
Lubricating oil	greases
Residue	asphalt

1. According to the data shown in Figure 1, crude oil enters the column at approximately:

   A. 170°C.
   B. 250°C.
   C. 350°C.
   D. 500°C.

2. Which of the following statements can be deduced from the information given?

F. Molecules with fewer carbon atoms have lower boiling points.

G. Molecules with fewer carbon atoms have higher boiling points.

H. Molecules with more carbon atoms have lower boiling points.

J. The number of carbon atoms does not affect the boiling point.

3. A fraction that is distilled at about 190°C is used for:

A. asphalt.

B. diesel fuel.

C. planes.

D. cars.

4. Which of the following is the best explanation for the use of bubble caps in the column?

F. To improve the efficiency of the distillation process

G. To lower the temperature of the distillation column

H. To slow the distillation process

J. To prevent destructive pressure build up in the column

5. Considering the makeup and uses of the listed hydrocarbons, it could be concluded from the information given that:

A. smaller hydrocarbons are slower than larger hydrocarbons.

B. larger hydrocarbons stick together better than smaller hydrocarbons.

C. smaller hydrocarbons stick together better than larger hydrocarbons.

D. larger hydrocarbons do not stick together.

PASSAGE II

Nitrogen is constantly recycled in nature. This process is called the *nitrogen cycle* and is shown in Figure 1.

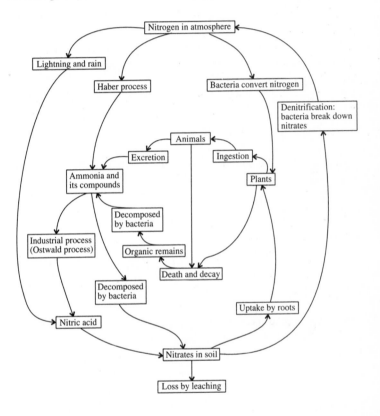

Figure 1

6. According to Figure 1, how do animals contribute to the nitrogen cycle?

F. Animal wastes and dead animals ultimately are decomposed and become nitrates in soil.

G. Through the Haber process their remains are turned into ammonia.

H. Dead animals and animal wastes immediately become nitrates in soil, are broken down by bacteria, and are released into the atmosphere.

J. Animals eat plants and convert plant protein into animal protein, which breaks down and is released into the air as protein-enriched nitrogen.

7. According to the data presented, nitrates in soil become nitrogen most directly by:

A. being absorbed by roots.

B. being broken down by bacteria.

C. being changed to ammonia.

D. forming nitric acid.

8. According to Figure 1, live animals will NOT be involved in the cycle:

F. if the plants they eat have not absorbed nitrates from the soil.

G. unless they die and are decomposed by bacteria.

H. only if they are involved in the Ostwald process.

J. unless their wastes ultimately become nitrates in soil.

9. Regardless of the route that is taken through the nitrogen cycle, which of the following is necessary to get nitrogen back into the atmosphere?

A. Nitrates in soil and bacteria

B. Ammonia and its compounds

C. Nitric acid

D. Dead animals and plants

10. Which one of the following must be involved in the Ostwald process?

F. Lightning and rain change nitrogen from the air into nitric acid.

G. Organic remains are decomposed by bacteria and become ammonia.

H. Ammonia and its compounds go through an industrial process, often becoming fertilizer.

J. Nitrogen is taken from the air and changed through the Haber process into ammonia and its compounds.

PASSAGE III

The owner of a large-scale salt-water tuna fishery wished to maximize the size of the tuna she produced, so she hired a marine biologist to conduct a series of experiments intended to discover what combination of four factors produces the best results. The fish farmer had determined that the size of the growing pool, the type of food available, the average water temperature, and the degree of salinity were the most important factors in raising the tuna fry to maturity and subsequent harvest and sale to market.

Up to this point, the farmer had kept the overall water temperature at 50°F, the salinity at 3.1%, and the pool size per 500 fry at 100,000 cubic feet, and she had the small tuna eating a medium amount of protein and a medium fat diet. Over the past ten growing seasons, her full-grown tuna had averaged 22.6 pounds per fish. These were her benchmark figures against which experimental results would be compared.

Four independent experiments were conducted. Each experiment varied only one of the four factors while keeping the other three at their benchmark levels. The data gathered by the marine biologist is shown in Tables 1 through 4.

Table 1	
Salinity (percent)	Average weight (pounds)
2.5	16.8
2.7	20.9
2.9	22.4
3.1	22.5
3.3	22.4
3.5	22.6
3.7	22.1
3.9	20.5

Table 2	
Temperature (°F)	Average weight (pounds)
40	23.4
45	23.2
50	22.7
55	22.7
60	22.8
65	22.6
70	22.1
75	20.5

Table 3	
Food Type (protein/ fat levels)	Average weight (pounds)
low/low	20.4
low/med	21.2
low/high	21.6
med/low	22.6
med/med	22.6
med/high	22.9
high/low	23.0
high/med	23.1
high/high	23.5

Table 4	
Pool size (per 500 fry/ cubic feet)	Average weight (pounds)
40,000	21.7
60,000	22.2
80,000	22.3
100,000	22.5
120,000	22.7
140,000	22.9
160,000	23.2
180,000	23.4

11. From the results of the experiments, it can be concluded that the farmer could do all of the following to increase the size of her mature tuna EXCEPT:

   A. increase the salinity to 3.5%.
   B. keep the temperature at a constant 50°F.
   C. increase the protein content of the food.
   D. give the fish more room in larger growing pens.

12. The validity of these experiments' data depends on the assumption that:

   F. factors in the fishes' environment can be manipulated.
   G. this variety of tuna can be effectively grown in captivity.
   H. the fishes can actually metabolize the high protein diet.
   J. the salinity of the water is not affected by the pool's size.

13. Based on the data, one can draw which of the following conclusions?

   A. Raising the temperature does not affect the size of the mature fish.
   B. A high-fat diet does not produce heavier fish.
   C. Enlarging the pool size will result in larger fish.
   D. Increasing the protein content of the food results in a greater expense for the farmer.

14. One could assume that which of the following groups of changes from the benchmark figures would likely maximize the size of the tuna produced?

   F. Adding salt, raising the temperature, raising protein/fat levels, enlarging the pool
   G. Reducing salt, lowering the temperature, raising protein/fat levels, enlarging the pool
   H. Adding salt, lowering the temperature, raising protein/fat levels, enlarging the pool
   J. Reducing salt, raising the temperature, lowering protein/fat levels, enlarging the pool

15. Of the four experiments, the one producing the least conclusive results is the one involving changes in:

   A. salinity.
   B. food type.
   C. temperature.
   D. pool size.

16. All of the following facts that would have a significant impact on the experiments are neglected EXCEPT:

   F. mortality rates.
   G. mineral and carbohydrate content of the food.
   H. pH of the seawater.
   J. density of the seawater.

PASSAGE IV

The *Richter scale* is used to measure the magnitude of earthquakes on a scale from 0 to 9. The earthquakes are measured in terms of amplitude and frequency of the surface waves. On the Richter scale, a quake measuring 2 is 10 times stronger than a quake measuring 1. A quake measuring 3 is 10 times stronger than a quake measuring 2, and so forth.

A researcher conducted studies of twelve different earthquakes on twelve different dates in nine different countries. He described the intensities of the quakes and listed the characteristic effects. He charted and graphed the information as shown in Table 1, Figure 1, and Table 2.

Table 1			
Study number	Date	Richter scale magnitude	Effect
1	Jan. 12	3.2	noticed only by a few people
2	Jan. 18	4.5	woke up those asleep
3	Jan. 23	2.1	detected by seismograph only
4	Mar. 2	6.8	houses collapsed
5	Mar. 4	5.7	walls cracked
6	May 25	4.1	objects moved
7	Jun. 4	3.7	heavy truck-type vibrations
8	Jul. 17	6.1	chimneys collapsed
9	Sep. 4	7.4	buildings and pipelines destroyed
10	Sep. 5	8.4	city totally destroyed
11	Oct. 15	7.1	landslides and ground cracked
12	Dec. 1	5.0	objects fell off shelves

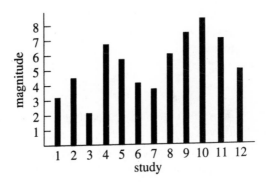

Figure 1

Table 2	
Magnitude	Description
less than 3.0	detected by instruments only
3.0 – 3.4	weak
3.5 – 3.9	slight
4.0 – 4.4	moderate
4.5 – 4.8	fairly strong
4.9 – 5.4	strong
5.5 – 6.0	very strong
6.1 – 6.5	destructive
6.6 – 7.0	ruinous
7.1 – 7.3	disastrous
7.4 – 8.1	calamitous
greater than 8.1	catastrophic

17. In Study 4, the magnitude would be considered:

    A. disastrous.

    B. calamitous.

    C. destructive.

    D. ruinous.

18. Which of the following could reasonably be assumed from the information given?

    F. Moderate quakes always occur in January.

    G. No walls crack during strong quakes.

    H. In a disastrous quake, chimneys are destroyed.

    J. The highest magnitude quakes occur in September throughout the world.

19. In how many studies did the quakes exceed the strength desig-
nated "fairly strong"?

   A. 6
   B. 7
   C. 8
   D. 9

20. A second researcher disputed the effects of the March 2 quake
and pointed to a flaw in the study and in the descriptions. Her
point of dispute would be strengthened if:

   F. it were pointed out that catastrophic quakes, although rare,
were also ruinous.
   G. she noted that landslides also made houses collapse.
   H. her research also showed that during a moderate quake on
March 2, some small objects rattled and almost fell.
   J. the study on March 2 was conducted in an area of poorly
constructed houses.

21. According to the information given in the twelve studies, the
effects caused by heavy trucks could:

   A. be detected only by instruments.
   B. be considered a slight vibration.
   C. wake up those who are asleep.
   D. crack thin walls.

22. The quake measured in Study 11 was approximately 100 times
greater than the quake measured on which of the following dates?

   F. January 18
   G. January 23
   H. July 17
   J. December 1

PASSAGE V

A *homologous series* is a series of organic molecules composed of a group of families with the same type of atoms, bonded in the same way to carbon atoms. The only difference in structure between molecules of different families in the series is the number of carbon atoms present. Although the physical properties change gradually in the series, the members share the same chemical properties. Alkanes, alkenes, and alcohols are all examples of homologous series, as shown in Table 1.

Table 1			
Homologous series	Number of carbon atoms		
	meth- 1	eth- 2	prop- 3
alkane	CH_4 meth<u>ane</u>	C_2H_6 eth<u>ane</u>	C_3H_8 prop<u>ane</u>
alkene	---------	C_2H_4 eth<u>ene</u>	C_3H_6 prop<u>ene</u>
alcohol	CH_3OH meth<u>anol</u>	CH_3CH_2OH eth<u>anol</u>	$CH_3CH_2CH_2OH$ prop<u>anol</u>

The simplest type of hydrocarbons are the alkanes. *Alkanes* are called saturated molecules because no more atoms can be added to them. The first three alkane molecules are reviewed in Table 2.

Table 2

Name	Number of carbon atoms	Formula	Structure	Boiling point (approx.)	Energy of combustion
methane	1	CH_4	H │ H–C–H │ H	–160°C	–890kJmol
ethane	2	C_2H_6	H H │ │ H–C–C–H │ │ H H	–90°C	–1,560kJmol
propane	3	C_3H_8	H H H │ │ │ H–C–C–C–H │ │ │ H H H	–40°C	–2,220kJmol

23. Based on the information given in Table 1, which of the following must be true?

   A. Methene is represented by CH_4.
   B. Propane has more carbon atoms than propene.
   C. Ethane and ethene have the same chemical properties.
   D. Ethanol and propanol have different physical properties.

24. Alcohols differ from alkanes and alkenes in that alcohols must contain:

   F. more carbon atoms than hydrogen atoms.
   G. more hydrogen atoms than carbon atoms.
   H. fewer carbon atoms than all other atoms.
   J. atoms other than carbon and hydrogen.

25. According to the information given in Table 2, which of the following graphs is the best representation of the relationship between the number of carbon atoms and the energy of combustion if the number of carbon atoms is plotted on the x-axis and the energy of combustion is plotted on the y-axis in a coordinate plane?

A.

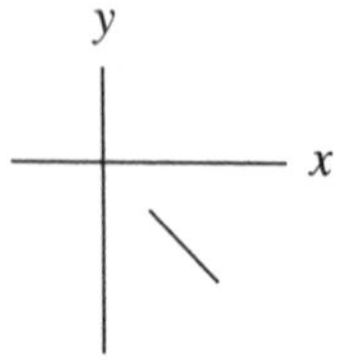

B.

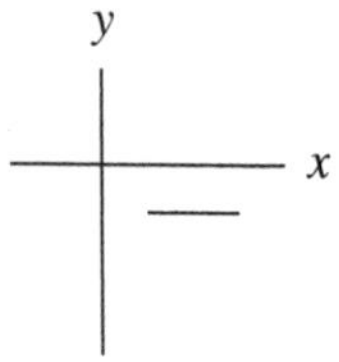

C.

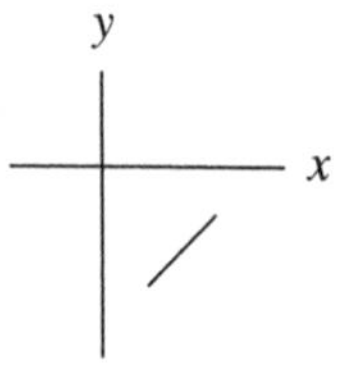

D.

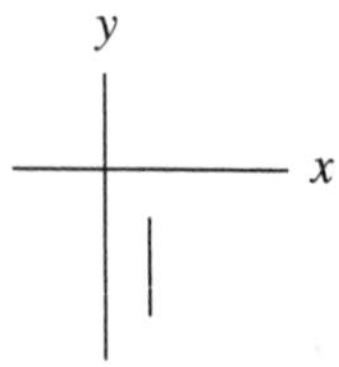

26. Based on a careful analysis of the data in Table 2, which of the following is the general formula for alkanes?

F. C_nH_{2n}

G. C_nH_{2n+2}

H. C_nH_{2n+4}

J. $C_{2n+2}H_n$

27. If alkanes can undergo substitution reactions, in which one atom swaps places with another atom, and if one of methane's hydrogen atoms swaps places with one chlorine atom from Cl_2, the outcome of chloromethane and hydrogen chloride would be represented by:

A. $CH_2Cl_2 + HCl$.

B. $CH_3Cl + HCl_2$.

C. $CH_3Cl + HCl$.

D. $CH_2Cl + H_2Cl$.

PASSAGE VI

A set of experiments was conducted to examine the relationship between resistors in parallel and series arrangements in direct current (DC) circuits. *Ohm's law* is given as $V = IR$, where V is the applied voltage given in volts, I is the observed current given in amperes (or amps), and R is the resistance of the circuit given in ohms. A researcher wishes to understand how the relationship of these resistors changes when multiple resistances in various configurations are considered. Four setups were employed in the experiments, and their *schematics,* or electrical diagrams, are shown in Figures 1 through 4. In these figures, the symbol next to the V,

$$\dashv||\vdash$$

corresponds to a battery or voltage source, the jagged, sawtoothed symbols are the resistors, and the circle with the A in it,

is an *ammeter,* a device used for measuring the current in the wire that connects the circuit.

Series circuit
2 resistors

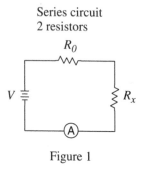

Figure 1

Series circuit
3 resistors

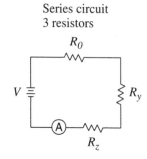

Figure 2

Parallel circuit
2 resistors

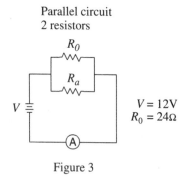

$V = 12V$
$R_0 = 24\Omega$

Figure 3

Parallel circuit
3 resistors

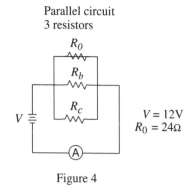

$V = 12V$
$R_0 = 24\Omega$

Figure 4

With the voltage V kept steady at 12 volts DC and R_0 kept at a constant 24 ohms, the other resistors were varied and the currents were measured after each change. The data were assembled and are shown in Table 1.

Table 1								
Data for Figures 1 through 4 (R given in ohms, I given in amps)								
Figure 1		Figure 2			Figure 3		Figure 4		
R_x	I	R_y	R_z	I	R_a	I	R_b	R_c	I
0	0.50	0	0	0.50					
1	0.48	1	1	0.46	1	12.5	1	1	24.5
2	0.46	2	2	0.43	2	6.5	2	2	12.5
4	0.43	4	4	0.38	4	3.5	4	4	6.5
6	0.40	6	6	0.34	6	2.5	6	6	4.5
8	0.37	8	8	0.30	8	2.0	8	8	3.5
12	0.33	12	12	0.25	12	1.5	12	12	2.5
24	0.25	24	24	0.17	24	1.0	24	24	1.5
36	0.20	36	36	0.13	36	0.83	36	36	1.2
120	0.08	120	120	0.05	120	0.60	120	120	0.70

28. Ohm's law, $V = IR,$ demonstrates what kind of variation between current and resistance?

   F. Direct variation

   G. Indirect variation

   H. Inverse variation

   J. Joint variation

29. The experimenter notices, after reviewing the data, that in series curcuits, when the sum of R_y and R_z equals R_x, the observed currents are roughly equal. What hypothesis would be a logical choice based on this analysis of the experiment?

   A. Resistances are additive in series circuits.
   B. Differing voltage sources produce differing currents.
   C. Observed currents in two different circuits can be made equal.
   D. Electric current follows the path of least resistance.

30. The circuits shown in Figure 3 and Figure 4 are called parallel circuits because:

   F. the opposite sides of the diagram are parallel.
   G. all of the resistors are positioned parallel to one another.
   H. each part of the circuit is shaped like a parallelogram.
   J. the voltage source side is parallel to the side without any resistors.

31. The most accurate graph of the relationship for the data obtained from Figure 1, with R being plotted on the x-axis and I on the y-axis, is:

   A.

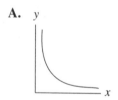

   B.

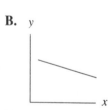

C. y

D. y

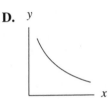

32. Which of the following is the most likely reason that the experimenter neglected to use zero values for resistors R_a, R_b, and R_c as was used with the resistors in the series circuits?

F. The experimenter had already collected that data in the series circuit phase of the experiment.

G. Using zero values for R_a, R_b, and R_c would result in a short circuit.

H. The observed current would be beyond the range of the ammeter.

J. The voltage source used would not be powerful enough to observe any current.

33. In the data collected from Figure 3, the ratio of R to I when R is 12 could be written as:

A. $12 : 1$.

B. $8 : 1$.

C. $4 : 1$.

D. $1 : 9$.

PASSAGE VII

During the development of the human embryo's brain and spinal cord, nerve growth and synaptic contacts occur with remarkable precision and selectivity. How do the right nerve connections get established in the first place?

Chemoelectric Theory:

Neural pathways are established and grow in response to electrical stimuli produced by instructions embedded in the genetic code. A specific set of logical impulses, not too dissimilar to a computer's series of ones and zeroes, allows or disallows certain pathways to be completed or not. The particular patterns of electrical impulses enhance or retard the chemical reactions that stimulate neuron growth. Of course, adequate nutrition is imperative; most notably in this regard, a reasonably high level of electrolytes is required to promote and sustain such growth.

Chemoaffinity Theory:

Complicated neural circuits are said to grow and organize themselves according to selective attractions between existing neurons, which are determined by chemical codes under genetic control. During early stages of their development, these neurons acquire individual chemical "identifications" by which they can reorganize and distinguish each other. The chemical specificity is precise enough to determine not only the postsynaptic cell to which the axon tip will grow but even the exact area on the postsynaptic cell that will be contacted. In addition to the proper necessary nutrients, the proper level of hormones must also be maintained.

Neural Frequency Theory:

It is known that each and every molecule has certain frequencies associated with it, naturally determined by the interatomic bonds within each molecule. These frequencies introduce vibrations within any medium with which they interact. Within the growing nervous system, specific frequencies are naturally produced as a function of genetic programming. In turn, these frequencies produce vibrations that are sympathetic to and support the formation of new compounds and combinations of compounds. Each of these precise vibrations corresponds to the growth mechanism of a specific type of cell; some produce muscle cells, some nerve cells and neuron growth, and so forth. As a human embryo develops, more and varied vibrations are introduced, which allow and promote cell differentiation. Not only are simple compounds allowed to form, but eventually the full range of neural pathways are literally grown in proper order according to instructions in the genetic code.

34. One way to approximate the activity assumed by the Chemoelectric Theory is to:

F. apply a constant low-level voltage across the body of a developing animal embryo.

G. apply an intermittent set of electrical impulses to an animal embryo.

H. increase the level of electrolytes to optimal levels within the embryo.

J. vibrate the embryo with a frequency characteristic of the enzyme acetylcholine.

35. Although the Chemoelectric Theory and the Chemoaffinity Theory differ, each implies the importance of:

A. proper nutrition.

B. a high level of electrolytes.

C. the proper level of hormones.

D. interatomic bonds.

36. Which theory does NOT at least imply the idea of neuron diversity?

   F. The Chemoelectric Theory
   G. The Chemoaffinity Theory
   H. The Neural Frequency Theory
   J. All of the theories discuss neural diversity.

37. Which of the following is a basic element included in all of the theories?

   A. Electrical stimuli
   B. Vibrations
   C. Selective attraction
   D. Genetics

38. If the Chemoaffinity Theory is correct, then which of the following is necessary?

   F. Chemical codes not under genetic control
   G. Maintaining the proper level of hormones
   H. Precise vibrations corresponding to growth mechanisms
   J. Maintaining a high level of electrolytes

39. An experiment was done in which the eyes of some young frogs were rotated 180 degrees from top to bottom after severing the optic nerve, which connects the eye to the brain. The results showed that when the nerves regrew, they established the new synaptic connections in their precisely ordered original position but that the visual image was upside down. Which theory does this experiment support?

   A. The Chemoelectric Theory
   B. The Chemoaffinity Theory
   C. The Neural Frequency Theory
   D. This experiment supports none of the three theories.

40. Which of the following would most weaken the Chemoelectric Theory?

    F. A study using inadequate nutrition also showed growth of neural pathways.

    G. A study using a low level of electrolytes also showed some neural growth.

    H. A study showed that neural pathways grow without any electrical stimuli.

    J. A study showed that logical impulses are not necessarily similar to a computer's series of ones and zeroes.

STOP. IF YOU FINISH BEFORE TIME IS UP, CHECK YOUR WORK ON THIS SECTION ONLY. DO NOT WORK ON ANY OTHER SECTION IN THE TEST.

SCORING AND COMPLETE ANSWERS AND EXPLANATIONS FOR THE PRACTICE TEST

Answer Key

English Test

Passage I

1. C
2. G
3. D
4. J
5. B
6. H
7. B
8. H
9. C
10. F
11. B
12. J
13. B
14. J
15. B

Passage II

16. F
17. D
18. F
19. B
20. F
21. C
22. H
23. D
24. J
25. C
26. J

27. B
28. H
29. C
30. H
31. C

Passage III

32. J
33. A
34. G
35. C
36. G
37. C
38. J
39. C
40. H
41. C
42. H
43. C
44. G
45. C

Passage IV

46. J
47. C
48. H
49. D
50. F
51. C
52. J

53. B
54. F
55. D
56. H
57. A
58. H
59. D
60. J
61. A

Passage V

62. F
63. B
64. G
65. C
66. J
67. A
68. H
69. A
70. G
71. D
72. F
73. C
74. J
75. C

Mathematics Test

1. C	31. E
2. J	32. G
3. D	33. B
4. H	34. K
5. B	35. C
6. H	36. H
7. B	37. D
8. F	38. G
9. C	39. B
10. G	40. K
11. C	41. A
12. H	42. J
13. A	43. D
14. J	44. J
15. C	45. A
16. J	46. G
17. D	47. B
18. J	48. F
19. B	49. A
20. F	50. F
21. B	51. D
22. H	52. G
23. A	53. B
24. H	54. G
25. E	55. A
26. J	56. G
27. D	57. C
28. H	58. H
29. D	59. B
30. F	60. K

Reading Test

Passage I

1. D
2. G
3. A
4. F
5. D
6. J
7. C
8. H
9. B
10. F

Passage II

11. A
12. J
13. D
14. F
15. B
16. F
17. C
18. G
19. A
20. H

Passage III

21. C
22. F
23. B
24. H
25. C
26. G
27. D
28. J
29. A
30. F

Passage IV

31. C
32. G
33. A
34. G
35. B
36. F
37. D
38. J
39. A
40. H

Science Reasoning Test

Passage I	Passage III	Passage VI
1. C	11. B	28. H
2. F	12. F	29. A
3. C	13. C	30. G
4. F	14. H	31. D
5. B	15. A	32. G
	16. J	33. B
Passage II		
6. F	Passage IV	Passage VII
7. B	17. D	34. G
8. J	18. H	35. A
9. A	19. B	36. F
10. H	20. J	37. D
	21. B	38. G
	22. J	39. D
		40. H
	Passage V	
	23. D	
	24. J	
	25. A	
	26. G	
	27. C	

Scoring Your ACT Practice Test

To score your practice test, total the number of correct answers for each section. Don't subtract any points for questions attempted but missed, as there is no penalty for guessing. This score is then scaled from 1 to 36 for each section and then averaged for the all-important composite score. The average score is approximately 18. To figure out your **percentage right** for each test, use the following formula. When you have your percentage right, use the charts on pages 12–13 determine your **approximate** scaled score.

English Test $\dfrac{\text{number right}}{75} \times 100 = \underline{\hspace{2cm}} \%$

Mathematics Test $\dfrac{\text{number right}}{60} \times 100 = \underline{\hspace{2cm}} \%$

Reading Test $\dfrac{\text{number right}}{40} \times 100 = \underline{\hspace{2cm}} \%$

Science Reasoning Test $\dfrac{\text{number right}}{40} \times 100 = \underline{\hspace{2cm}} \%$

Analysis Chart

	Reason for Mistake				
	total missed	simple mistake	misread problem	lack of knowledge	lack of time
English					
Mathematics					
Reading					
Science Reasoning					
Total					

Analysis/Tally Chart for Problems Missed

One of the most important parts of test preparation is analyzing **why** you missed a question so that you can reduce the number of mistakes. Now that you've taken the practice test and checked your answers (be sure to read all the answer explanations that follow before completing this chart), carefully tally your mistakes by marking them in the proper column.

Reason for Mistake

	total missed	simple mistake	misread problem	lack of knowledge	lack of time
English					
Mathematics					
Reading					
Science Reasoning					
Total					

Reviewing all of the information above should help you determine why you're missing certain questions. Now that you've pinpointed the type of error, you'll be aware that you must focus on avoiding that type of error on the actual test.

1. **C** The sentence has no subject or verb, only the participle *join-ing*. Both choices **C** and **D** correct this error, but the separation of the verb and its object in choice **D** is awkward.

2. **G** The clause *observers agree* is parenthetical (a parenthetical phrase or clause is one that interrupts the flow of the sentence and that could be omitted without changing the meaning of the sentence). So the phrase must be set off with two commas, one before and one after.

3. **D** The phrase *of his era* means of the time or in that period, so it isn't necessary to repeat the information as choices **A, B,** and **C** do.

4. **J** If you read only the first sentence of this paragraph, the past perfect tense (*had won*) of the original sentence appears to be correct. But when you've read the whole paragraph, you see that it uses the past tense (*was, grew up, won*) in the other sentences. To make the first sentence consistent with the rest of the paragraph, you must use the past tense (*won*).

5. **B** The best choice to introduce a list is the colon. The semicolon usually comes between two complete sentences. You could use a comma after *sports,* but you also need a comma after *baseball,* so choice **C** is incorrect.

6. **H** The easiest way to order the paragraph is chronologically. Begin with his childhood [2], then his growing up [3], then his college years [1], then the time *after graduating* [4].

7. B The phrase *his wife* is an appositive (a word or phrase that identifies another). It should be set off with commas before and after. The appositives in choices **C** and **D** are both punctuated incorrectly.

8. H The first two elements in this series have verbs in the past tense (*raised* and *continued*). This third clause must have a parallel verb in the past tense (*became*). Since the *she* isn't repeated in the second clause, it shouldn't be repeated in the third.

9. C The most concise way to add this detail is with the clause introduced by *which*. Choice **C** is better than **D** because it avoids the wordiness of *purpose and function* and the pompous diction of *academic endeavors*. As a rule, a paragraph of only one sentence, choice **A,** should be avoided.

10. F This past perfect tense (*had ended*) is the correct form to indicate an action completed before the action of the past tense (*entered*) in the main clause, although you could also use the past tense (*ended*).

11. B The sense of this sentence and that of the preceding one make it clear that the transitional opening phrase should indicate a continuation rather than a contradiction as choices **A, C,** and **D** suggest.

12. J The awkward and wordy clause of the original should be revised to this straightforward version. Choice **G** is a sentence fragment, and **H** uses a verb in the present tense, while the rest of the paragraph uses only the past tense.

13. B The correct punctuation to divide two closely related independent clauses is the semicolon.

14. J The fourth and fifth paragraphs can be combined easily. The fourth is already short, and both deal with Robinson's career after his retirement from baseball.

15. B To eliminate the third paragraph is the best choice here. The subject of the essay is Jackie Robinson, not his wife.

PASSAGE II

16. F The correct punctuation between two independent clauses is a semicolon.

17. D Since *difficult* and *hard* and *hard to do* all have the same meaning, you need only the one word *difficult.* To use two is to be redundant.

18. F The present tense is the correct choice here; the verb describes the condition now. The singular is also correct. Although *the Netherlands* looks like a plural, it's a collective noun that's treated as a singular, like *the United States.*

19. B In this context, you could use the noun *diversification* (but not *by diversification*), but the best choice is the infinitive *to diversify.*

20. F The original sentence is correctly punctuated. The colon is the best choice to introduce a list, and the first two items in the list should be set off by commas. The semicolon is sometimes used to separate the parts of a series but only when the elements of the series have internal commas.

21. C The present tense is consistent with the verb tenses in the rest of the paragraph, but the subject is the plural *types,* so the verb should be the plural *account.*

22. **H** This added sentence is an appropriate conclusion of the paragraph and makes clear its relation to the main issue of the essay, the competition with foreign growers. Since diversification hasn't solved the problem, the essay must logically go on to other steps. If sentence **F** were included, it should go before what is now the last sentence, not after it. Sentence **G** tells you that five percent from one hundred leaves ninety-five, but chances are, you already know that. Sentence **J** fits better after the first sentence of the paragraph than after the last.

23. **D** The verbs *look* and *appear* are linking verbs and are followed by an adjective, not an adverb. The right answer here is the simplest: *look good.*

24. **J** This clause is the third part of a series, and the first two elements aren't clauses but compound nouns: *disease resistance* and *crop yield.* The best choice should be parallel to the other parts of the series; *shelf-life* is synonymous with *how long a tomato will keep* but also is a compound noun that sustains the parallelism.

25. **C** Since the sentence is about a disease of tomatoes, it would most logically follow the sentence that mentions *disease resistance,* the third.

26. **J** The phrase *they say* is parenthetical and should have commas on both sides.

27. **B** The phrase is the last part of a series of five verb phrases in which the subject (*tomatoes*) isn't repeated. To maintain the parallelism, you must use only a verb with the subject the understood *tomatoes.* The choices that include *they* can't be right.

28. H The phrase *a dud in the market* is colloquial, and it is a metaphor, but it is still the best (and the liveliest) choice here. The punctuation tells you that the sentence is an exclamation, and *a dud in the market* is suitably exclamatory. It is also neatly parallel to *tomato in the field.* The word *marketwise* (if there is such a word) is the advertising jargon of the midcentury. Choice **G** uses the awkward and wordy *as a tomato,* and the bland word choice of **J** is a very odd exclamation. You must be aware of consistency in the tone of your language, but there are times when the colloquial is better than overly formal language.

29. C In this context, the comparative form (*more*) of the adverb (*carefully*) should be used to modify the verb *tended.*

30. H Since the *workers* are humans, the correct pronoun here is *who.* Use *who* rather than *whom,* since the pronoun is the subject of *who can harvest ground-grown tomatoes only once.*

31. C This is neither a personal nor an argumentative essay. There is never any sense of an opposing view or any attempt by the author to tell about himself or herself. Its subject is agriculture and economics.

PASSAGE III

32. J The sentence begins with the participial phrase *Based on the principle that learning can take place outside a classroom.* All but one of the possible answers follow with *the students* or *students.* But it isn't the students who are based on principle; it's the new university. Only choice **J** places the modified noun next to the phrase that modifies it.

33. **A** The original version is correct, rightly parallel to *some in off-campus locations.* Choice **B** breaks the parallelism with an extra *and,* while **C** adds an unnecessary *are offered.* Choice **D** changes the meaning.

34. **G** The possessive here requires an apostrophe. Since *term* is a singular, the correct form is *term's.*

35. **C** The *Nonetheless* here suggests a contradiction, but the sentence carries on the listing of things that are not found on this campus. Of the four introductory words or phrases, only *In fact* fits this context.

36. **G** To be consistent with the rest of the paragraph, the verb tense must be present. To agree with the plural subject *athletics,* the verb must be *are.*

37. **C** The sentence is, as choice **C** explains, a good topic sentence that gives a rationale for the details that follow. As a conclusion, the sentence would not follow reasonably from the sentence about the grandmother who is student body president. Choice **B** is unconvincing, since the sentence would explain the details of the paragraph whether it came at the beginning or the end.

38. **J** The subject that follows the initial prepositional phrase, *Unlike the University of Florida or Florida State,* is *continuing education.* The modifying phrase that begins with *Unlike* must refer to something that can be unlike continuing education, such as a policy, as in choice **J,** but not a university, as in choices **A, B,** and **C.**

39. C This phrase could be set off with two dashes, with two commas, or within parentheses, so choices **B, C,** and **D** are possible. The *that is* must also be set off with a comma, but since the comma is missing in choices **B** and **D,** the right answer is **C.**

40. H The paragraph is about the university's concern with continuing education and environmental studies. The water birds nearby are only remotely related to the issues of the paragraph and even farther from the subject of the essay as a whole.

41. C The possessive of the pronoun *it* is spelled *its,* without an apostrophe. *It's* is a contraction for *it is.* Here, to agree with the singular *location,* the correct choice is *its.*

42. H *They're* is the contraction of *they are,* while *their* is a possessive form. The correct word here is *there.*

43. C The word should be enclosed in quotation marks and followed by a comma between the two independent clauses.

44. G The word the pronoun refers to here is *communities.* Since the antecedent isn't a person, the pronoun *which,* not *who,* should be used. Choice **H** isn't wrong, but it's a wordier way of saying the same thing.

45. C Choice **C** includes most of the major issues of the essay: the varied kinds of instruction, the concern for local students, and the range in the ages of the students. The other choices touch on fewer of the subjects of the essay.

PASSAGE IV

46. J Since the phrase *As the twentieth century draws to a close* defines the present, it is redundant to say *at this time, at the present,* or *now.* The best version of the sentence avoids the repetition.

47. C The subject of the verb is *most,* a singular as it is used in the phrase *most of the coyote population.* To agree, the verb must be the singular *was confined.* In this context, the idiomatic preposition with *confined* is *to* rather than *in,* restricted to rather than shut up in.

48. H Choices **G** and **J,** which simply give examples of states or countries, while not wrong, are uninteresting additions, and the information of **F** might have been supposed. Choice **H** adds information that has human interest and provides a motive for wishing to eradicate the coyote.

49. D This is another example of redundancy. A *cause* is what makes something happen, brings it about, or makes it occur; all of the three phrases repeat what has already been said.

50. F The original phrase is correct. *More cunning* is the correct comparative form for the adjective. The omission of the word *ever* in choice **H** changes and weakens the meaning, which is that the generations grow increasingly more intelligent.

51. C The original version, using only the demonstrative pronoun *This,* is obscure, since *This* refers to a word in another sentence, while *This increase* is immediately clear.

52. J The sentence can be written *a single coyote, it is said, has killed* with commas on both sides of the interrupting phrase and an active verb in place of the infinitive (*to have killed*). The only correct choice here, **J**, leaves out the *it* and the internal punctuation: *a single coyote is said to have killed.*

53. B The problem here is the placement of this modifier. If it's omitted, the sentence loses an important meaning. Of the choices, the best is **B**, which makes it clear that seven hundred sheep were killed in three years.

54. F The original is the right version. *Fiercely* is an adverb used to indicate how very toxic the compound is. To change the adverb to an adjective (*fierce*) distorts the intended meaning.

55. D The *that* and *which* distinction is a minor issue here, but the major grammatical error is the lack of a subject in this relative clause. Only choice **D** adds the missing subject (*it*) and the correct singular verb (*causes*).

56. H There are two independent clauses here. They must be separated by either a semicolon dividing a single sentence or a period dividing two.

57. A Of the four choices, only the *But* suggests a change of direction. The sense of this sentence, set against the preceding paragraph, should make it clear that the new paragraph will present opposition to the poisons.

58. H The wordy phrase *Due to the fact that* should always be replaced; the single word *because* says the same thing. The first part of this sentence is a subordinate clause, so you can't say only *Collars.*

59. D This sentence weakens the paragraph and should be deleted. It isn't relevant to the subject of the paragraph, which is the toxicity of the chemicals, not the eating habits of the coyote.

60. J This is another redundancy. Since *century* means one hundred years, *over a century,* and *more than one hundred years* say the same thing.

61. A The original is punctuated correctly and is more direct than choice **C,** the only other choice that has the needed question mark.

PASSAGE V

62. F The passage is correctly punctuated. The three words that are quotations are properly set in quotation marks, there are no commas after *"pure"* and *"uncluttered,"* and the sentence ends with a period. It isn't necessary to use commas when three items are separated by *or . . . or.* If the sentence read *"pure, uncluttered, and clean"* or *"pure," "uncluttered," and "clean,"* the commas would be needed.

63. B The phrase *as some psychologists suggest* is parenthetical and should be set off with a comma before and after. Choice **C** isn't wrong, but this passive (*is suggested*) is a wordier construction.

64. G The phrase can be either *that is perceived to be* or *that is perceived as being.* No comma should interrupt the phrase. To say only *that is* changes the meaning to an assertion of the greater confidence and optimism of the fifties, while the original sentence says only that the fifties are supposed to have been more confident (but perhaps they really weren't).

65. C The correct idiom with the comparative is *more than.* It isn't ungrammatical to repeat the *more,* but it's wordier and unnecessary. Given the choice, **C** is better.

66. J The original version has an agreement error (*is* with *doors*), and choice **G** has only a participle, but no main verb. Choice **H** is grammatical, but **J** is preferable, as it saves two words, the useless *There are.*

67. A The semicolon is the best choice to separate two related independent clauses, although you could write two sentences and use periods. You should set off the introductory phrase *as a rule* with a comma.

68. H The word *Inside* makes the transition from the exteriors of the second paragraph (*the lines, the roof*) to the interior, and the rest of this sentence introduces the inexpensive materials such as Formica and plywood. The addition of this sentence would improve this rather short paragraph.

69. A The placement of the adverb *just* next to *coming* is correct. Choices **C** and **D** are grammatical, but they miss some of the meaning of the original phrase.

70. G The first sentence of this paragraph uses the verb *are built.* While it isn't wrong to use the same verb in the next sentence, if an appropriate alternative is available, it's better to have some variety. Choice **F** can't be right because both *are built* and *are constructed* are passive. Choice **H** is ridiculous. In fact, good writers probably choose the shorter word more often than the longer one. Choice **J** is also a weak answer because the meanings of *built* and *constructed* are alike.

71. D The solution here is to place the phrase *in Pennsylvania* so that it is close to the *house on a waterfall*. Choice **D** is the only one that does so.

72. F The third paragraph is about the indoors, the fourth about the outdoors, so the sentence does made the transition clear. The next three sentences are examples of what this sentence describes. Choice **G** isn't wrong, but it isn't as complete an answer as **F**. Both choices **H** and **J** are simply untrue.

73. C The sentence begins with the participle *Furnished*. This initial participial phrase must be followed by what it modifies, something that is *furnished*. But *the end of the war,* choice **A**, or a *construction boom,* **B**, or a *small boom,* **D**, can't be *furnished*. The correct answer must be **C**, which begins with *modern houses,* the subject that the participial phrase modifies.

74. J There isn't enough difference in meaning between *approached* and *came near* to make the use of both of them necessary. Choice **J** is the best, since it's the most concise.

75. C The first sentence mentions a *small number of discerning homeowners,* and the last echoes this phrase with its *small but enthusiastic group.* All three of the other answers offer reasons that are simply untrue.

1. **C** 30% of 40 is $.30 \times 40 = 12$. That is, 12 students in the class of 40 students are math majors. If 12 students are math majors, then $40 - 12 = 28$ students who are not math majors.

2. **J** In the figure, the sum of $\angle ABC$ and 30 must be 180. So $\angle ABC$ is $180 - 30 = 150°$.

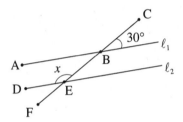

Because ℓ_1 is parallel to ℓ_2, $\angle ABC$ must be equal to $\angle DEB$. So $\angle DEB$, which is x, must also be 150°.

3. **D** If the average on three tests is 80, the total score on these three tests is $80 \times 3 = 240$ (because the total is the number of items times their average). If the score on the fourth test is 70, the total score on all four tests is $240 + 70 = 310$. Then the average for all four tests is

$$\text{average} = \frac{310}{4} = 77.5$$

4. **H** If 30% of the mountain's height is 6,000 feet, then 1% of its height in feet is

$$\frac{6,000}{30} = 200$$

So 50% of the height is $200 \times 50 = 10,000$ feet.

5. B The distance between $-6°$ and $22°$ is

$$22 - (-6) = 22 + 6 = 28$$

(Notice that it is *not* 16.) Half this distance is 14. So Q is 14 degrees more than -6 (or 14 degrees less than 22), which is $8°$.

6. H Because the four sides of a square have equal lengths, the length of each side of the square is one quarter of the perimeter. So if the perimeter of the square is 24, its length must be 6 and its area must be $6 \times 6 = 36$, which is also the area of the rectangle (because you're told that the rectangle and the square have equal areas).

You know that the length of the rectangle is 4 times its width. So if the width is w, the length must be $4w$. Then

$$\text{area of rectangle} = w \times 4w$$

$$36 = 4w^2$$

$$\frac{36}{4} = w^2$$

$$9 = w^2$$

$$3 = w$$

If the width is 3, then the length must be $3 \times 4 = 12$. Then

$$\text{perimeter of rectangle} = 2(l + w)$$

$$= 2(12 + 3)$$

$$= 30$$

7. B You know

$$8 - 2p = 16$$

Subtracting 8 from both sides, you get
$$-2p = 8$$

Dividing both sides by -2, you get

$$p = -4$$

Subtracting 8 from both sides, you get
$$p - 8 = -4 - 8$$
$$= -12$$

8. F If you first collect the a terms from the numerator and denominator, you get

$$\frac{(-5a)^2}{25a^3} = \frac{25a^2}{25a^3} = \frac{1}{a}$$

Similarly, collecting the b terms, you get

$$\frac{-3b^3}{-9b^2} = \frac{b}{3}$$

And collecting the c terms, you get

$$\frac{(2c^2)^3}{6c^5} = \frac{8c^6}{6c^5} = \frac{4c}{3}$$

Multiplying the three terms, you get

$$\frac{1}{a} \cdot \frac{b}{3} \cdot \frac{4c}{3} = \frac{4bc}{9a}$$

9. **C** In 1997, the company's total revenue was $20,000. In 1998, this amount dropped by 15%. You know that 10% of 20,000 is 2,000 (move the decimal one place to the left) and 5% is half of this, which is 1,000. So 15% of 20,000 is 2,000 + 1,000, or 3,000. So the 1998 revenue is $3,000 less than $20,000, which is $17,000. Alternatively, you could simply use your calculator.

10. **G** $x \cdot |3 - 5| = x \cdot |-2|$. The absolute value of -2 is 2 (remember that the absolute value is always positive). So

$$x \cdot |3 - 5| = x \cdot 2$$

You're given that $x = -|2|$, which means that $x = -2$. Then

$$x \cdot |3 - 5| = -2 \cdot 2 = -4$$

11. **C** If 20% of the marbles are red and 60% are blue, that means that 80% of the marbles are either red or blue and that the remaining 20% of the marbles are green. Since you know that 24 marbles are green and that the total number of red marbles equals the total number of green marbles (because the number of marbles of each color equals 20%), there are 24 red marbles.

12. **H** To find the least common multiple of 8, 12, and 16, you can take the multiples of the largest number (16) and see which is the smallest one that is divisible by the other two numbers (8 and 12). Multiples of 16 are 16, 32, 48, 64, etc. Of these, the smallest number that is divisible by both 8 and 12 is 48. So the least common multiple of the three numbers is 48.

The factors of 8 are 1, 2, 4, and 8. The factors of 12 are 1, 2, 3, 4, 6, and 12. The factors of 16 are 1, 2, 4, 8, and 16. So the greatest common factor of 8, 12, and 16 is 4.

You need to find the *difference* between the least common multiple (48) and the greatest common factor (4), which is

$$48 - 4 = 44$$

13. A The distance between points A and B is 4 (notice that A is 1 unit to the left of the y-axis and B is 3 units to the right of the y-axis). This means that one side of the rectangle is 4. Therefore, the opposite side, $\overline{CD}$, is also 4, and the sum of these two sides is then 8.

If the perimeter of the rectangle is 18, the sum of the two remaining sides should be $18 - 8 = 10$. So each of the sides should be $10 \div 2 = 5$. So $\overline{AC}$ should be 5 units long.

Notice that A is 2 units above the x-axis. So point C should be 3 units below the x-axis (so that $\overline{AC}$ is 5). So the y-coordinate of point C is -3. Note that only one answer choice, choice **A**, has -3 as the y-coordinate.

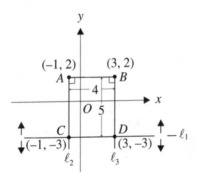

14. J Notice that $(x - y)$ is common to all the terms except the last one, which is $-3(y - x)$. But you can change the last term, since you know that $-3(y - x) = +3(x - y)$. So

$$(x - y)[5(x - y) - 3(y - x)]$$
$$= (x - y)[5(x - y) + 3(x - y)]$$
$$= (x - y)[8(x - y)]$$
$$= 8(x - y)(x - y)$$
$$= 8(x - y)^2$$

15. C Since $\angle GBF$ is 130°, $\angle EBF$ is 50° (because together they make up a line). You know that $\angle BEF$ is 90° (because it's given as a right angle). If $\angle EBF$ is 50°, then $\angle EFB$ must be 40° (because $180 - (90 + 50) = 40$).

Because $\angle EFB$ and $\angle CFD$ are vertically opposite angles, $\angle CFD$ must also be 40°. You know that $\angle FCD$ is 90° (because right angle BCA and $\angle FCD$ must sum to 180°).

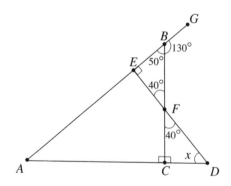

Therefore,

$$x = 180 - (90 + 40)$$
$$= 180 - 130$$
$$= 50$$

16. J The slope of a line is given by the formula

$$\text{slope} = \frac{y_2 - y_1}{x_2 - x_1} \quad \frac{\text{(change in } y)}{\text{(change in } x)}$$

From (3, 4) to (7, 1), you can simply plug into the formula.

$$\text{slope} = \frac{1-4}{7-3} = \frac{-3}{4}$$

17. D Since 20% of 100 is 20, the discounted price of the stereo is $100 - 20 = \$80$. The sales tax is 8% of this amount. That is, the sales tax is $.08 \times 80 = \$6.40$. So the total price for the stereo is $80 + 6.40 = \$86.40$.

18. J If the area of $\triangle ABC$ is 20 square inches, you can write

$$\tfrac{1}{2} \times \text{base} \times \text{height} = 20$$

If you take $\overline{AB}$ as the base and $\overline{BC}$ as the height, then

$$\tfrac{1}{2} \times 5 \times \overline{BC} = 20$$

Multiplying each side by 2 gives

$$5 \times \overline{BC} = 40$$

Now, dividing each side by 5 leaves

$$\overline{BC} = 8$$

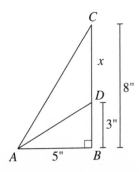

If $\overline{BC}$ is 8 and, as shown in the figure, $\overline{BD}$ is 3, then $\overline{CD}$ must be $8 - 3 = 5$ inches.

19. **B** Since Sean spent 60% of his earnings on music CDs, he had 40% remaining. So if x is the total earnings, the amount remaining after purchasing the music CDs was 40% of x, or $.40x$. He spent 80% of this amount on clothes. That is, he spent 80% of $.40x$ on clothes, which is $.80(.40x)$. So the amount he spent on clothes is

$$.80(.40x) = .32x$$

20. **F** If you multiply the second expression, $(5p - 2q^2)$, by p, you get $5p^2 - 2pq^2$. And if you multiply the second expression, $(5p - 2q^2)$, by $-q^3$, you get $-5pq^3 + 2q^5$.

Then adding the two new expressions, you get
$$5p^2 - 2pq^2 - 5pq^3 + 2q^5$$

A couple of notes about this problem: First, be careful about the negative sign in front of the q^3 in the first expression, $(p - q^3)$. Also, remember that q^3 times q^2 is q^5, not q^6.

You could also use the FOIL method (first, outer, inner, last) to multiply the two binomials.

$$(p \;-\; q^3)(5p \;-\; 2q^2)$$

$$5p^2 - 2pq^2 - 5pq^3 + 2q^5$$

21. B You know that the cost of a notebook is 4 times the cost of a pencil. That is, if n is the cost of a notebook and p is the cost of a pencil, then $n = 4p$.

You're told that 3 pencils and 2 notebooks cost $2.20. That is,
$$3p + 2n = 2.20$$

If you substitute $n = 4p$ in this equation, you get
$$3p + 2(4p) = 2.20$$
$$3p + 8p = 2.20$$
$$11p = 2.20$$

Now, dividing by 11 gives
$$p = 0.20$$

So the cost of the pencil is $0.20. You could also work this problem from the answers.

22. H If there are 1,760 yards in a mile and 1 mile is 1.6 kilometers, then there must be 1,760 yards in 1.6 kilometers. That is,

$$1.6 \text{ kilometers} = 1,760 \text{ yards}$$
$$1 \text{ kilometer} = \frac{1,760}{1.6} \text{ yards}$$
$$= \frac{17,600}{16} \text{ yards}$$
$$= 1,100 \text{ yards}$$

Since 1 kilometer $= 1,100$ yards, then
$$2 \text{ kilometers} = 2 \times 1,100 = 2,200 \text{ yards}$$

Or you could set up the proportion
$$\frac{1,760}{1.6} = \frac{x}{2}$$

and solve.

23. A Jan is 15 years older than Sue. If you let J be Jan's age now and S be Sue's age now, you can write

$$J = S + 15$$

In 5 years, Jan's age will be $J + 5$ and Sue's will be $S + 5$. You know that Jan will be twice as old as Sue. Then

$$J + 5 = 2(S + 5)$$

Replacing J with $S + 15$,

$$S + 15 + 5 = 2S + 10$$
$$S + 20 = 2S + 10$$
$$20 = S + 10$$
$$10 = S$$

So Sue is 10 years old.

24. H The number of bacteria is

$$N = 1 + 1.5t + 25t^2$$

If you want to find the number of bacteria 10 seconds after they are first collected, you should plug in 10 as the value of t in the equation. Then

$$N = 1 + 1.5(10) + 25(10^2)$$
$$= 1 + 1.5(10) + 25(100)$$
$$= 1 + 15 + 2,500$$
$$= 2,516$$

25. E The perimeter of the figure is the sum of all the sides. You know the lengths of all sides except $\overline{BC}$ and $\overline{CD}$. If you draw $\overline{BD}$, you see that it is 8 feet (because $\overline{AE}$ is 8 feet). Then if F is the midpoint of $\overline{BD}$ (creating right triangle BFC), $\overline{BF} = \overline{FD} = 4$ feet. You know that point C is 13 feet from $\overline{AE}$ and that   is 10 feet. So $\overline{CF}$ should be $13 - 10 = 3$ feet.

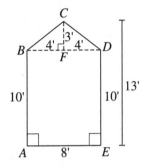

Then in right triangle *CFB*, $\overline{BF} = 4$ feet and $\overline{CF} = 3$ feet. Then using the Pythagorean theorem, you get

$$c^2 = a^2 + b^2$$
$$\left(\overline{BC}\right)^2 = \left(\overline{CF}\right)^2 + \left(\overline{BF}\right)^2$$
$$\left(\overline{BC}\right)^2 = 3^2 + 4^2$$
$$= 9 + 16$$
$$\left(\overline{BC}\right)^2 = 25$$
$$\overline{BC} = 5$$

Then the perimeter of the figure is

$$\text{perimeter} = \overline{AB} + \overline{BC} + \overline{CD} + \overline{DE} + \overline{EA}$$
$$= 10 + 5 + 5 + 10 + 8$$
$$= 38$$

26. J Notice that there are four tick marks and five spaces separating 3 and 4. So each tick mark represents $\frac{1}{5}$, or 0.2. *P* is between the third and fourth tick mark. The value of the third tick mark is 3.6, and the value of the fourth tick mark is 3.8. So *P* should be more than 3.6 and less than 3.8. Of the given choices, 3.7 (or 3.70) is the closest.

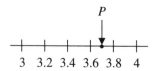

27. D You know that $\frac{1}{3}$ is about .33 and $\frac{2}{3}$ is about .67. So you need to find a number that is in the interval .33 to .67.

Choice **A** $\frac{4}{5}$ is .8, so it lies outside the given interval.

Choice **B** $\frac{3}{4}$ is .75, which also lies outside the interval.

Choice **C** $\frac{5}{6}$ is about .83, which also lies outside the interval.

Choice **D** $\frac{2}{5}$ is .4, which *does lie inside the interval.*

Choice **E** $\frac{2}{7}$ is about .29, which also lies outside the interval.

So only choice **D** lies inside the given interval.

28. H To find the area of $\triangle CED$, you need its base, $\overline{DE}$, and its height, $\overline{CE}$. Notice that because *ABCD* is a rhombus, and because side $\overline{AB}$ is 4, all sides of the rhombus must also be 4. Furthermore, because $\overline{AB}$ is parallel to $\overline{DC}$, $\angle CDE$ is also 30°. Then in $\triangle CED$, $\angle D = 30°$ and $\angle E = 90°$. So $\angle C$ must be 60°, which means that $\triangle CED$ is a 30°– 60°– 90° triangle.

CLIFFS QUICK REVIEW

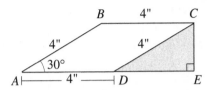

In a $30°-60°-90°$ triangle, the three sides are in the ratio 1 to $\sqrt{3}$ to 2 (opposite the $30°, 60°,$ and $90°$ angles, respectively). Because side $\overline{CD}$ (which is opposite the $90°$ angle) is 4, each side of the triangle must be 2 times the $1:\sqrt{3}:2$ ratios. So side $\overline{DE}$ (which is opposite the $60°$ angle) is 2 times $\sqrt{3}$, that is, $2\sqrt{3}$, and side $\overline{CE}$ is 2 times 1, which is 2.

Then the area of $\triangle CED$ is

$$\text{area} = \tfrac{1}{2} \times \text{base} \times \text{height}$$
$$= \tfrac{1}{2} \times 2\sqrt{3} \times 2$$
$$= 2\sqrt{3}$$

29. D When people are given 3 red marbles each, there are 2 red marbles remaining, which means that the total number of red marbles (R) should be 2 more than a multiple of 3.

Similarly, the total number of green marbles (G) should be 2 more than a multiple of 5 because people are given 5 green marbles each and 2 green marbles remain.

In choice **A,** $R = 16$, which is only 1 more than a multiple of 3 (because 15 is a multiple of 3). So choice **A** can't be the correct answer.

In choice **B,** $R = 20$, which is 2 more than a multiple of 3. So it could be the answer. But $G = 33$, which is 3 more than a multiple of 5. So choice **B** can't be the correct answer.

In choice **C,** $R = 17$, which is 2 more than a multiple of 3, but $G = 28$, which is 3 more than a multiple of 5. So choice **C** can't be the correct answer.

In choice **D,** $R = 32$, which is 2 more than a multiple of 3, and $G = 52$, which is 2 more than a multiple of 5. It looks as though this choice could be the correct answer. Here, $N = 10$. If 10 people are given 3 red marbles each and there are 2 more red marbles remaining,

$$R = 3 \times 10 + 2 = 32$$

Similarly, if 10 people are given 5 green marbles each and there are 2 more green marbles remaining,

$$G = 5 \times 10 + 2 = 52$$

So choice **D** is the correct answer.

30. F Notice that a triangle with sides of 9, 12, and 15 is a 3–4–5 triangle in which each side has been multiplied by 3. It is also a right triangle with hypotenuse 15.

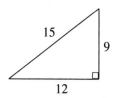

This triangle has a base of 12 and a height of 9 (or vice versa). So its area, in square units, is

$$\tfrac{1}{2} \times \text{base} \times \text{height} = \tfrac{1}{2} \times 12 \times 9$$
$$= 54$$

31. E To find the point of intersection, note that the x and y values of the point must satisfy both equations. So to find the point, you can equate the two equations.

$$5x - 3 = 2x + 6$$

Adding 3 to both sides gives

$$5x = 2x + 9$$

Next, subtract $2x$ from each side, and you have

$$3x = 9$$

Finally, divide each side by 3 leaving

$$x = 3$$

If you notice that only choice **E** has 3 as the value of x, you know that this has to be the right answer and you don't need to do any more work. If you don't notice that fact, your next step would be to plug this value of x into either of the two equations to find the value of y, which works out to be 12, since $5(3) - 3 = 15 - 3 = 12$. So the coordinates are (3, 12).

32. G The equation of the given line is $3y = -4x + 12$.

First you should plot this line. To do so, set x equal to 0. Then you get

$$3y = -4(0) + 12$$
$$= 12$$

Now dividing by 3 gives

$$y = 4$$

Since $y = 4$, (0, 4) is the point at which the line intersects the y-axis. Now, if you set y equal to 0, you get

$$3(0) = -4x + 12$$
$$0 = -4x + 12$$

Now add $+4x$ to each side and you have
$$4x = 12$$

Dividing each side by 4 leaves
$$x = 3$$

So $(3, 0)$ is the point at which the line intersects the x-axis. You can draw the line as shown in the diagram.

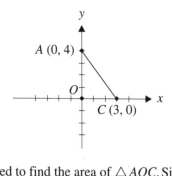

You now need to find the area of $\triangle AOC$. Since $\overline{OC} = 3$ and $\overline{OA} = 4$, the area is
$$\text{area of triangle} = \tfrac{1}{2} \times 3 \times 4$$
$$= 6$$

33. B Let l_A and w_A represent the length and width of rectangle A. And let l_B and w_B represent the length and width of rectangle B. Because you know that the two areas are equal, you can write

Or
$$l_A \times w_A = l_B \times w_B$$

$$\frac{l_A}{w_B} = \frac{l_B}{w_A}$$

But since

$$\frac{l_A}{w_B}$$

is given as $\frac{2}{1}$, you have

$$\frac{2}{1} = \frac{l_B}{w_A}$$

You need to find the ratio of the width of rectangle A to the length of rectangle B, so simply invert each ratio in the proportion above. So

$$\frac{1}{2} = \frac{w_A}{l_B}$$

Therefore, the required ratio is 1 : 2.

34. K You know that distance $=$ rate $\times$ time. Time is h hours for both cars. For car P, the speed is p, so distance traveled by car P in h hours is ph. For car Q, the speed is q, so the distance traveled by car Q in h hours is qh. So the total distance traveled by the two cars is $ph + qh$, which equals $h(p + q)$.

35. C The given inequality is
$$2x < 4x - 8$$

Subtracting $4x$ from both sides of the inequality, you get
$$-2x < -8$$

Dividing by -2, you get
$$x > 4$$

(Remember that when you multiply or divide an inequality by a negative number, you have to reverse the sign of the inequality.)

The graph of the solution set of $x > 4$ is best represented by choice **C**.

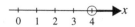

Notice that choice **E** is incorrect because it represents $x \geq 4$.

36. **H** To find the overall average, you can simply add the weighted scores. Gino scored 50 on the first test, which is to be weighted 30%. Then the contribution of the first test toward the overall average is $.30 \times 50 = 15$.

Similarly, the second test score is also weighted 30%. So the contribution of the second test toward the overall average is $.30 \times 70 = 21$.

And the contribution of the third test is $.40 \times 90 = 36$.

So the overall average is $15 + 21 + 36 = 72$.

37. **D** To find the perimeter of the triangle, you need to find the lengths of the three sides. You see that $\overline{AC} = 3$ inches. You now need to find $\overline{AB}$ and $\overline{BC}$.

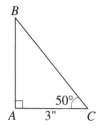

Using AB to mean the measure of $\overline{AB}$ and BC to mean the measure of $\overline{BC}$, you know that

$$\cos 50° = \frac{AC}{BC} = \frac{3}{BC}$$

Substituting the given value of $\cos 50°$, you get

$$.64 = \frac{3}{BC}$$

which means

$$\frac{.64}{1} = \frac{3}{BC}$$

Now cross multiplying gives

$$.64BC = 3$$

So, using your calculator,

$$BC = \frac{3}{.64} = 4.69$$

and

$$\sin 50° = \frac{AB}{BC} = \frac{AB}{4.69}$$

Substituting the given value of $\sin 50°$, you get

$$.77 = \frac{AB}{4.69}$$

or

$$.77 \times 4.69 = AB$$
$$3.61 \approx AB$$

Then the perimeter of the triangle is

$$\overline{AB} + \overline{BC} + \overline{AC} = 3.61 + 4.69 + 3 = 11.3$$

The closest approximation is 11.5.

38. G You know that x is an integer, which means that p should be a factor of 60 (so that when you divide 60 by p, there is no remainder). Furthermore, you know that p is a prime number. There is one more condition: x has to be the smallest possible integer, under the conditions stated, which means that p should be as large as possible. So you need to find the largest factor of 60 that is also a prime number.

Factors of 60 are 1, 2, 3, 4, 5, 6, 10, 12, 15, 20, 30, and 60. Of these, the largest prime number is 5. So the smallest value of x is

$$\frac{60}{5} = 12$$

39. B Because points A, B, and C are on one line, you know that the sum of the angles shown must be $180°$. That is,
$$x + y + y + x = 180°$$

You also know that $2x = y$. Substituting this value of y, you get
$$x + y + y + x = 180°$$
$$x + 2x + 2x + x = 180°$$
$$6x = 180°$$

Now dividing by 6 leaves
$$x = 30°$$

40. K If a line touches the y-axis 4 units above the x-axis, the y-intercept of the line must be 4. Also, when $x = 0$, $y = 4$.

The equation of a line is $y = mx + b$, where b is the y-intercept. In this problem, b must be 4, so the y-intercept is 4.

Choice **F** $y = 4x$ means that the y-intercept is 0.

In choice **G**, if the equation $4y = x$ is divided by 4, you get

$$y = \frac{x}{4}$$

which also has a y-intercept of 0.

If you rearrange choice **H** $4x + y = 0$, you get $y = -4x$, which also has a y-intercept of 0.

If you rearrange choice **J** $4y + x = 0$, you get

$$y = \frac{-x}{4}$$

which also has a y-intercept of 0.

Choice **K** $y = x + 4$ has 4 as the y-intercept, so it is the correct answer.

Another method is to say the coordinates $(0, 4)$ must make the equation of the line true. So you can plug these coordinates into the answer choices to see which is true.

41. A In an equilateral triangle, all three sides are of equal length. So if the perimeter of one of the smaller equilateral triangles is 3, then each of its sides is 1.

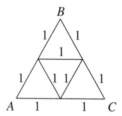

The perimeter of $\triangle ABC$ is the sum of $\overline{AB}, \overline{BC}$, and $\overline{CA}$. $\overline{AB}$ is made up of 2 sides of length 1 each. So $\overline{AB}$ is 2. Similarly, $\overline{BC}$ is 2 and $\overline{CA}$ is 2. Therefore, the perimeter of $\triangle ABC$ is

$$2 + 2 + 2 = 6$$

42. J The given triangle is a right triangle, and y is the hypotenuse.

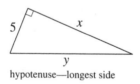

hypotenuse—longest side

Since y is the hypotenuse, it must be the longest side, so you can eliminate any choice in which y is not greater than 5. So you can eliminate choices **F** and **G.** You can also eliminate choice **K,** since y is not the longest side in this choice. Now, using the Pythagorean theorem,

$$c^2 = a^2 + b^2$$
$$y^2 = x^2 + 5^2$$

You can try the remaining choices to see which one works in the formula.

Choice **H**:

$$y^2 = x^2 + 5^2$$
$$15^2 \stackrel{?}{=} 10^2 + 5^2$$
$$225 \neq 100 + 25$$

Choice **J**:

$$y^2 = x^2 + 5^2$$
$$13^2 \stackrel{?}{=} 12^2 + 5^2$$
$$169 = 144 + 25$$

This is correct, so choice **J** has to be the right answer.

43. D You might sketch the following figure to help you.

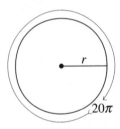

You know that the circumference of a circle is $2\pi r$, where r is the radius. You're given that the circumference is 20π feet. Then

$$2\pi r = 20\pi$$

Dividing each side by 2π gives

$$r = 10$$

The area of a circle is πr^2. If the radius is 10, the area is

$$\text{area} = \pi r^2 = \pi(10^2) = 100\pi$$

---

44. J To find the difference of matrices A and B, subtract the corresponding entries as follows:

$$\begin{bmatrix} 4 & -1 \\ 3 & 1 \end{bmatrix} - \begin{bmatrix} 5 & -1 \\ -4 & 2 \end{bmatrix} \qquad \begin{matrix} 4-5=-1 & -1-(-1)=0 \\ 3-(-4)=7 & 1-2=-1 \end{matrix}$$

So the correct answer is

$$\begin{bmatrix} -1 & 0 \\ 7 & -1 \end{bmatrix}$$

which is choice **J.**

45. A You know that the perimeter of a rectangle is given by

$$\text{perimeter} = 2(l+w)$$

where l is the length and w is the width. You're given that the perimeter is 22. Then

$$22 = 2(l+w)$$

Dividing each side by 2 leaves

$$11 = l + w$$

If the width is 4, the length must be

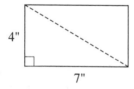

4"

7"

So the length is 7 and the width is 4. The area of the largest triangle enclosed by the rectangle is half the rectangle's area. The area of the rectangle is $7 \times 4 = 28$, which means that the area of the triangle, in square inches, is 14.

46. G The coordinates of point P are $(x, 3x)$, which means that the y-coordinate (in this case, $3x$) is always 3 times the x-coordinate. Notice also that within the shaded region, the y-coordinate is always greater than 3 times the x-coordinate.

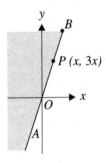

To find the coordinates of a point that lies outside the shaded region, you should look for a point whose y-coordinate is less than 3 times the x-coordinate.

Choice **F:** $x = -1, y = -1$ (y is greater than $3x$)

Choice **G:** $x = 1, y = 1$ (y is less than $3x$)

Choice **H:** $x = -2, y = -3$ (y is greater than $3x$)

Choice **J:** $x = -2, y = -4$ (y is greater than $3x$)

Choice **K:** $x = 3, y = 10$ (y is greater than $3x$)

So only choice **G** has its y-coordinate less than $3x$, which means that this point lies outside the shaded region.

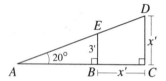

47. B

Using $AB, AC, BC,$ and BE as the measures of $\overline{AB}, \overline{AC}, \overline{BC},$ and $\overline{BE}$, respectively, first, consider $\triangle ABE$. In it,

$$\tan 20° = \frac{BE}{AB}$$

Substituting the value of $\tan 20°$, you get

$$\frac{9}{25} = \frac{3}{AB}$$

Cross multiplying gives

$$9(AB) = 75$$

And dividing by 9 leaves

$$AB = \frac{75}{9}$$

Next, in $\triangle ACD$, you have

$$\tan 20° = \frac{x}{AC}$$

Since $AC = AB + BC$, then

$$\frac{x}{AC} = \frac{x}{(AB + BC)}$$

Substituting $\frac{75}{9}$ for AB and x for BC gives

$$\frac{x}{(AB + BC)} = \frac{x}{\frac{75}{9} + x}$$

Since this is equal to $\tan 20°,$ which is $\frac{9}{25}$ you have

$$\frac{9}{25} = \frac{x}{\frac{75}{9} + x}$$

Now, by cross multiplying you get

$$9\left(\tfrac{75}{9} + x\right) = 25x$$
$$75 + 9x = 25x$$

Subtracting $9x$ from each side gives

$$75 = 16x$$

Dividing by 16 leaves

$$x = \frac{75}{16} \approx 4.7$$

Choice **B** 4.8 is the closest approximation.

48. **F** Remember, $\log_x x$ is always 1. That is, if the base of the logarithmic function is the same as the number whose logarithmic value is being calculated, the logarithmic value equals 1. So $\log_2 2 = 1$. Now, substituting into the expression gives

$$\log_2(\log_2 2 + \log_2 2) = \log_2(1+1) = \log_2(2) = 1$$

49. **A** For a person 65 inches tall, the recommended weight, according to the formula is

$$\text{recommended weight} = 2.2(\text{height}) + 6$$
$$= 2.2(65) + 6$$
$$= 143 + 6$$
$$= 149$$

Since Raul weighs 160 pounds, he is $160 - 149 = 11$ pounds overweight.

50. F Because the radius of the semicircle is 2, $\overline{OA}$ (which is a radius) and $\overline{OB}$ (another radius) are each 2. Because $\overline{OA} = \overline{OB}$, $\angle ABO$ must also be 30°. This means that $\angle AOB$ must be 120° (so that the three angles in the triangle add up to 180°).

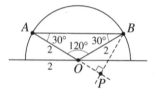

To find the area of $\triangle OAB$, you need its base and its height. If you take $\overline{AO}$ as the base (which is 2) and extend $\overline{AO}$ to P such that $\overline{BP}$ is perpendicular to $\overline{AP}$, then $\overline{BP}$ is the height of the triangle.

In $\triangle BPO$, $\angle BOP$ must be 60° (because $\overline{AP}$ is a line and $\angle BOA$ is 120°) and $\angle BPO$ is 90°. This means that $\angle PBO$ must be 30°. So $\triangle BPO$ is a 30°– 60°– 90° triangle.

In a 30°– 60°– 90° triangle, the sides are in the ratio 1 to $\sqrt{3}$ to 2. Notice that side $\overline{BO}$ (which is opposite the 90° angle) is 2, which means that $\overline{BP}$ (which is opposite the 60° angle) must be $\sqrt{3}$.

So the base of $\triangle AOB$ is 2 and the height is $\sqrt{3}$. So the area is

$$\text{area} = \tfrac{1}{2} \times \text{base} \times \text{height}$$
$$= \tfrac{1}{2} \times 2 \times \sqrt{3}$$
$$= \sqrt{3}$$

51. D You know that the radius of the area enclosed by the ripple doubles every second. At time $= 2$ seconds, the radius is 5 feet. Then at time $= 3$ seconds, the radius will be 10 feet. At time $= 4$ seconds, the radius will be 20 feet. And at time $= 5$ seconds, the radius will be 40 feet. So

$$\text{surface area} = \pi r^2 = \pi(40)^2 = 1{,}600\pi$$

52. G To answer this question, it would be helpful to construct the following chart.

	Ride Bikes	**Take Bus**	**Total**
Boys	A	B	.40
Girls	C	D	.60
Total	.30	.70	1.00

You need to find the quantity in cell C above. Notice that to find the quantity in any cell, you simply multiply the two corresponding marginal probabilities (one from the row and the other from the column). So cell C is

$$.60 \times .30 = .18$$

53. B You know that the cost of manufacturing 250 pencils is t dollars. Then

$$\text{cost of manufacturing 1 pencil} = \frac{t}{250}\text{dollars}$$
$$= \frac{t \times 100}{250}\text{cents}$$
$$= \frac{2t}{5}\text{cents}$$

You also know that it costs p cents for the lead for each pencil. Since the lead costs twice as much as the wood,

$$\text{cost of wood for 1 pencil} = \frac{p}{2}\text{cents}$$

Together, the lead and the wood for 1 pencil cost

$$p + \frac{p}{2} = \frac{2p}{2} + \frac{p}{2}$$

$$= \frac{3p}{2}\text{cents}$$

This is the total cost of manufacturing a pencil, which can be equated with the cost of manufacturing (one pencil) you found earlier. So

$$\frac{2t}{5} = \frac{3p}{2}$$

Cross multiplying gives

$$4t = 15p$$

And dividing by 4 leaves

$$t = \frac{15p}{4}$$

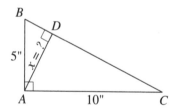

54. G

Notice that

$$\text{area of } \triangle ABC = \tfrac{1}{2} \times \text{base} \times \text{height}$$

$$= \tfrac{1}{2} \times 10 \times 5$$

$$= 25$$

Using the Pythagorean theorem you can find $\overline{BC}$ as

$$c^2 = a^2 + b^2$$
$$\left(\overline{BC}\right)^2 = \left(\overline{AB}\right)^2 + \left(\overline{AC}\right)^2$$
$$= 5^2 + 10^2$$
$$= 25 + 100$$
$$\left(\overline{BC}\right)^2 = 125$$
$$\overline{BC} = \sqrt{125}$$
$$= 5\sqrt{5}$$

You can also find the area of $\triangle BAC$ by considering $\overline{BC}$ as the base and $\overline{AD}$ as the height. Then

$$\text{area of } \triangle BAC = \tfrac{1}{2} \times \text{base} \times \text{height}$$
$$= \tfrac{1}{2} \times \overline{BC} \times \overline{AD}$$

Now, substituting the area of the triangle as 25 and $\overline{BC}$ as $5\sqrt{5}$, you get

$$25 = \tfrac{1}{2} \times 5\sqrt{5} \times \overline{AD}$$
$$50 = 5\sqrt{5} \times \overline{AD}$$
$$\frac{50}{5\sqrt{5}} = \overline{AD}$$
$$\frac{10}{\sqrt{5}} = \overline{AD}$$

Multiplying the numerator and denominator by $\sqrt{5}$, you get

$$\frac{10\sqrt{5}}{\sqrt{5}\sqrt{5}} = \overline{AD}$$

$$\frac{10\sqrt{5}}{5} = \overline{AD}$$

$$2\sqrt{5} = \overline{AD}$$

Since $x = \overline{AD}, x = 2\sqrt{5}$.

55. A Since each toss is independent of the next, and the probability of each outcome is $\frac{1}{2}$, you would multiply $\frac{1}{2} \times \frac{1}{2} \times \frac{1}{2} \times \frac{1}{2}$, which equals $\frac{1}{16}$.

56. G If the average score of 5 students is 6, the total score must be $5 \times 6 = 30$. The median score (5) is the third highest score. so if you arrange the scores in an increasing order, this is what you know so far:

$$\overline{\underset{A}{}} \quad \overline{\underset{B}{}} \quad \overset{5}{\underset{C}{}} \quad \overline{\underset{D}{}} \quad \overset{15}{\underset{E}{}} \quad \text{Total} = 30$$

Because the total is 30, $A + B + D$ must be 10 because the other two scores add up to 20. Furthermore, D must be an integer greater than 5 (because 5 is the median and no two scores are equal). To make the second highest score (D) as large as possible, you need to make A and B as small as possible. So if $A = 1$ and $B = 2$, and $A + B + D = 10$, then $1 + 2 + D = 10$, so $D = 7$.

57. C You're given

$$3x + y = 15$$

If you multiply each term in this equation by 1.5, you get

$$4.5x + 1.5y = 22.5$$

Notice that this is exactly what you need to find.

58. H To find the coordinates of the center of the ellipse, set $(x + 4)$ equal to 0 and $(y - 2)$ equal to 0 and solve each equation. It is evident that $x = -4$ and $y = 2$. So the center of the ellipse is $(-4, 2)$.

59. B Using the figure below, you can see that the length of the longest stick will be $\overline{PD}$.

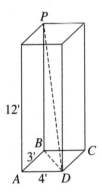

To find $\overline{PD}$, you first need to find the length of $\overline{BD}$. Given that $\overline{AB} = 3$ and $\overline{AD} = 4$, and using the Pythagorean theorem, you have

$$c^2 = a^2 + b^2$$
$$\left(\overline{BD}\right)^2 = \left(\overline{AB}\right)^2 + \left(\overline{AD}\right)^2$$
$$= 3^2 + 4^2$$
$$= 9 + 16$$
$$\left(\overline{BD}\right)^2 = 25$$
$$\overline{BD} = 5$$

Now you have another right triangle, $\triangle PBD$, in which $\overline{BP}$ is 12 and $\overline{BD}$ is 5. Then

$$c^2 = a^2 + b^2$$
$$\left(\overline{PD}\right)^2 = \left(\overline{BP}\right)^2 + \left(\overline{BD}\right)^2$$
$$= 12^2 + 5^2$$
$$= 144 + 25$$
$$\left(\overline{PD}\right)^2 = 169$$
$$\overline{PD} = 13$$

So the longest stick that could fit in the room would be 13 feet long.

60. K According to the given rules, the first character can be any letter of the alphabet, of which there are 52 (26 lower-case letters and 26 upper-case letters), any number from 0 to 9, of which there are 10, the pound sign, or the dollar sign. That is, the number of possibilities for the first character is

$$52 + 10 + 2 = 64$$

Similarly, the second character can be chosen from 64 possibilities. Then the total number of possibilities is 64 for the first character times 64 for the second character and so forth through the eighth character. That is, the total possibilities equal

$$64 \times 64 \times 64 \times 64 \times 64 \times 64 \times 64 \times 64 = 64^8$$

Since 64 is the same as 2^6, you can write 64^8 as $(2^6)^8$, or 2^{48}.

1. D Since Carrie is traveling from her hometown through Wisconsin to Chicago, she is obviously midwestern. Also, see lines 50–51. Choice **A** is incorrect (see lines 50–51), and nothing suggests the family is socially ambitious, choice **B**. Although the passage implies that her father is hard-working, nothing indicates the family is uncaring, choice **C**.

2. G These lines suggest a slight nervousness; Carrie is thinking that she *can* return home if things don't work out. Although she is both naïve, choice **F,** and ignorant of many things, choice **H,** these aren't revealed in the lines cited. Choice **J** is simply incorrect.

3. A The author interrupts the present action to comment on the fate of young girls coming to the city. *Angry diatribe* is too strong, choice **B.** The passage isn't ironic, choice **C;** the author isn't criticizing small-town attitudes. Choice **D** is incorrect; small-town life isn't described or contrasted with city life.

4. F See lines 29–34. All of the other answers are possible (and even common) ways of viewing the city, but you should stay with what is presented in the passage.

5. D Statement III is the only correct description. Carrie has a *certain native intelligence,* and she has an unformed prettiness rather than beauty. Also, Carrie doesn't have a strong will; she is described as timid; notice that she vacillates about talking to the man on the train.

6. J Earlier the author uses the seducer metaphor to describe the city. Here, in a clever turn, he shows Carrie thinking of the city as *groveling* at her slipper. The pronoun *it* in line 60 refers to the *mysterious city* in line 59; therefore, the phrase in this question can't refer to choices **F, G,** or **H.**

7. C See lines 68–72. Carrie has some maidenly reserve and hesitates, making choice **A** incorrect. Lines 85–86 show Carrie's youthful inexperience, making choice **B** also incorrect. Although Carrie may indeed long for wealth and position, that longing is not shown in this particular exchange, choice **D.**

8. H He is smooth, not embarrassed, choice **F,** and he says the words in *a pleasing way.* He isn't poking fun at her, choice **J.** At this point in the conversation, he hasn't said anything that could be construed as a lie, choice **G.**

9. B According to the picture of Carrie presented and the author's comments in the third paragraph on the dangers of the city, **B** is the best choice. Carrie is *unformed, ignorant*—hardly a strong, ambitious manipulator, choice **A.** She is also a mixture of average abilities, innocence, and vanity, not destined to be a positive influence on people she meets, choice **C.** From the third paragraph, you can see that Carrie may become a victim; she is too slight a character to become a tragic heroine, choice **D,** even though what happens to her may be sad.

10. F The author neither condemns nor elevates Carrie; he shows both her positive traits and her flaws. He isn't affectionate, choice **G** (notice descriptions such as *insipid prettiness* and *mind rudimentary in its power*). However, *disgusted,* choice **H,** is too strong to describe his tone. The view of Carrie is straightforward, not ironic, choice **J.**

PASSAGE II

11. A See lines 3–4. It is reasonable to assume that there would be changes in law and custom between tenth- and twentieth-century England. The author doesn't indicate the relative importance of inherited traits or goods, choice **B.** She doesn't suggest the term shouldn't be used for genetic inheritance, choice **C.** Choice **D** is also incorrect; the passage states that tangibles are generally passed on when someone dies. *Tangible* means can be touched.

12. J See lines 16–17. Choices **F** and **G** aren't suggested in the paragraph. Choice **H** might be a tempting choice, but the author notes that it is a change in *attitude* toward inherited wealth that has led to high taxation; she doesn't make a judgment about the difficulty of taxation.

13. D See lines 10–12. Choice **A** is incorrect; see the last paragraph of the passage. The problem with choice **B** is the use of the word *always;* the passage mentions exceptions from both the past and the present. Choice **C** is correct but is a minor point and therefore not the best contrast.

14. F See lines 21–23. Choice **G** is incorrect; land was bought and sold, but its normal route from one person to another was inheritance. Neither choice **H** nor **J** is supported by any evidence in the passage.

15. B Knighthood was previously a social status that was always inherited. Both choices **A** and **D** are material inheritances, whereas nobility of character, choice **C,** is a personal asset that at one time was believed to be hereditary.

16. F See lines 33–34. Money and personal property (choices **G** and **J**) are often passed from parents to children today, but that is by choice rather than by law. Positions in the church, choice **H,** were never inheritable by law.

17. **C** The author isn't making judgments about the validity of legal or customary inheritance here, choice **A,** nor is she contrasting customs in different countries, choice **D.** Such a contrast is irrelevant in this passage. The example illustrates social, not material, inheritance, choice **B.**

18. **G** See lines 57–59. Choices **F, H,** and **J** reflect various attitudes toward the relationship between heredity and environment, but none reflects the author's explanation for the examples shown in lines 59–67.

19. **A** *Hierarchical* can describe church organization, choice **C,** but here it refers to a society based on class. Although the author contrasts this society to a more democratic one, *hierarchical* is not a synonym for *totalitarian,* choice **D.** The author is contrasting a society based on the equality of all people with a society based on class. Although such a society may seem rigidly archaic, choice **B,** this perception is not implicit in the definition of *hierarchical.*

20. **H** See lines 66–71. Although choice **F** may be accurate, the author doesn't address the issues of education and opportunity. Choice **G** is addressed, but it isn't the author's main point. Choice **J** is incorrect; no such genes are suggested by the author, who implies that the belief that attitudes are inherited is obsolete.

PASSAGE III

21. **C** Leonardo used oil, and Verrocchio used egg tempera (lines 4–8). Enamel-like colors are a characteristic of egg tempera, making choice **B** incorrect. Choice **D** is also incorrect; Leonardo didn't disregard perspective, and more important, perspective isn't mentioned in the first paragraph. Although choice **A** might be true, the author doesn't make such a judgment in this paragraph.

22. F See lines 10–13. Choices **G** and **H** aren't suggested in the paragraph. Although Leonardo's use of a new medium is mentioned, nothing indicates that Verrocchio disapproved, choice **J**.

23. B See lines 19–20. Realism isn't judged, choice **A,** and it is linear—not aerial—perspective that Brunelleschi developed, choice **D**. Choice **C** is simply an incorrect understanding of perspective as it is used in the passage.

24. H See lines 24–26. Choice **F** defines linear perspective rather than the aerial perspective used by Leonardo. Combining media, choice **G,** isn't related to perspective, and choice **J** isn't relevant to Leonardo's technique as it is described in the passage.

25. C See lines 27–33. According to the passage, Leonardo's use of aerial perspective in this work isn't particularly impressive, making choice **A** incorrect. Although the background *prefigures* the *Mona Lisa,* it isn't the same, choice **B**. Choice **D** isn't indicated by the author. He doesn't compare Leonardo with his contemporaries here.

26. G Choice **G** is stated directly in lines 40–44. It is Botticelli, not Michelangelo, who Leonardo says isn't well rounded, choice **F**. No mention in this passage is made of Leonardo's criticizing Michelangelo's landscapes, choice **H**. Choice **J** is contradicted in lines 40–44.

27. D Leonardo doesn't comment on Botticelli's use of perspective, choice **A,** or accuse him of being a careless painter, choice **B**— except perhaps in his landscapes. The idea of the sponge was Botticelli's way of emphasizing the unimportance of landscapes, not a description of his techniques, choice **C**. It was the attitude and *very sorry landscapes* that Leonardo criticized.

28. **J** Both Leonardo's comments on Botticelli and his *Treatise on Painting* show his interest in other artists and in theories of painting. The passage also makes it clear (lines 10–13) that he experimented in his own works. Nothing in the passage supports choices **F** or **H,** and choice **G** is in fact contradicted by Leonardo's notes and his treatise.

29. **A** Note the adjective *varnish-clouded.* Earlier in the passage (lines 2–4) is evidence that choice **D** is incorrect, and choice **C** would refer to a problem not related to Leonardo's technique—which the description (*overpainted, varnish-clouded*) emphasizes.

30. **F** The paragraph moves after the first sentence to Botticelli's idea of studying a random patch. Leonardo's interest in this idea was as a source of inspiration, not as a valid defense of the unimportance of landscapes, choice **G.** The paragraph doesn't summarize, choice **H,** or compare Hugo's work to Leonardo's, choice **J;** it only mentions Hugo's use of the random-patch idea.

PASSAGE IV

31. **C** Summarizing the problems caused by internal-combustion cars prepares for the passage's main point. The paragraph doesn't cover developments in automotive efficiency, and the tone isn't critical, choice **A.** Other nations' not accepting the U.S. contribution to climatic change, choice **D,** is mentioned only in the last sentence. Choice **B** may seem the best, but the passage covers more than the relationship between cars and global climatic change—urban pollution, depletion of resources, and inflation of fuel prices.

32. G See lines 18–27. The passage states that even with the high price of fuel, 80 percent of passenger travel in Europe is by car, choice **H,** and no contrast with the use of mass transit in the United States is cited. Also, no point is made about the difference in fuel prices, choice **F.** The author is illustrating a point with this example; he isn't advocating anything, choice **J.**

33. A See lines 29–33. Methanol could be introduced at relatively low cost (lines 30–31), so choice **B** is incorrect. Choice **C** isn't covered in the passage. Although the oil companies are spending billions to develop better gasoline, nothing in the passage mentions that they are spending billions to lobby against methanol, choice **D.**

34. G See lines 41–47. Choice **F** is incorrect; the author mentions *entrenched advantages of gas-powered cars.* Choice **H** is also incorrect; the passage indicates that people haven't been willing to make significant changes or sacrifices for a clean environment. Also, the passage doesn't imply that cost is the only concern of consumers, choice **J.**

35. B See lines 18–22. Neither the effect on fuel prices, choice **A,** nor the need for developing countries to increase vehicle use, choice **C,** is covered. The passage indicates that reduction of vehicle use would have far more than marginal effects on the environment, choice **D,** but that the idea is impractical because people will simply not reduce their driving.

36. F An internal-combustion car, unlike an electric car, relies on a constantly running engine (lines 58–62). Nothing in the passage indicates that the electric car has less power, choice **G,** or that electric cars use alternative fuels, choice **J.** Regenerative braking schemes, choice **H,** are part of electric-drive, not internal-combustion, vehicles.

37. **D** In context, choices **A** and **B** don't make sense. The root of the word is the same as the root for *motion,* not *power,* choice **C**.

38. **J** See line 79. Choice **F** refers to the percent of energy in its storage cells that an electric motor converts to motion. Choice **G**, 25 percent, is the percent of energy in gas that an internal-combustion car converts to motion. The difference between those numbers, choice **H**, might appear to be the net efficiency advantage of an electric motor, but it doesn't take into account the relatively poor efficiency of the system that charges the electric motor's storage cells.

39. **A** See lines 80–84. Choice **B** is incorrect; an electric car already consumes no energy while at rest or coasting. Choice **C** refers to fuel cells, which have nothing to do with combined-cycle generation. Choice **D** is incorrect; the exhaust heat is from a power plant, not a car.

40. **H** The author says that developments in computer and military technology have already affected the viability of electric cars (lines 42-47). Changing to electric cars isn't inevitable, choice **F**, but requires a *concerted effort.* Choice **G** is also incorrect; carpooling and use of mass transit have decreased since World War II. Also, nothing suggests that oil companies will develop alternative fuels, choice **J**, only that they will work on making gasoline less polluting.

1. **C** Notice that the crude oil enters the fractional distillation column from the lower left. Since it enters the column between the 300 and 400 degree level and the 400 and 500 degree level, the best approximation is about 350°C.

2. **F** From Figure 1 it can be seen that refinery gas has the lowest boiling point and the fewest number of carbon atoms. Gasoline has a few more carbon atoms and a slightly higher boiling point. Reviewing all of the fractions will prove that molecules with fewer carbon atoms have lower boiling points.

3. **C** From Figure 1 it can be seen that kerosene is distilled at about 190°C. Considering the data in Table 1, you can see that kerosene is used for planes.

4. **F** Information given with Figure 1 shows that bubble caps are domes that "deflect the rising oil vapor onto trays" from which the fraction is piped off. You can reason that bubble caps make the column more efficient.

5. **B** From the information given in Figure 1 and Table 1, you can see that the fraction with the greatest number of carbon atoms (residue) is used for asphalt, which must stick together well. A careful comparison of the number of carbon atoms in each fraction and its uses shows that it could be expected that as the hydrocarbons get smaller (fewer carbon atoms), the fractions do not stick together as well.

PASSAGE II

6. **F** According to the diagram, animal excretion (wastes) and dead animals are ultimately decomposed by bacteria and then become nitrates in the soil.

7. **B** The most direct way that nitrates in soil become nitrogen is by denitrification (being broken down by bacteria thereby releasing nitrogen back into the air).

8. **J** By following the diagram, you can see that for live animals to be in the cycle, their wastes must ultimately become nitrates in soil.

9. **A** Working backward along the right side of the diagram, you can see that the only way to get nitrogen back into the air is through the steps of nitrates in the soil and denitrification (bacteria breakdown).

10. **H** The only path in the diagram that actually goes through the industrial process (Ostwald process) is choice **H**. Ammonia and its compounds go through an industrial process that generally produces fertilizer.

PASSAGE III

11. **B** Examining the results of the data will verify that the changes described in choices **A, C,** and **D** do, in fact, enlarge the size of the mature tuna.

12. **F** From the opening passage, it's clear that the farmer's initial intent was to find which combination of variables produces the heaviest fish. If such variables could not be manipulated, there would be no reason to perform these experiments.

13. C From the data, you can see that enlarging the pool size will result in larger fish. A high-fat diet, choice **B**, may or may not produce heavier fish (depending on its combination with protein). Although choice **D** is probably true, that conclusion is not displayed in the data.

14. H From the data, it is clear that the combination of adding salt (changing salinity to 3.5), lowering the temperature, raising protein/fat levels (to high/high), and enlarging the pool would be likely to maximize the size of the tuna. Each of these items increases the size.

15. A The results in the salinity experiments are the least consistent in the effect on the final weight of the fish. The other experiments show a more consistent increase or decrease.

16. J Since the salinity and temperature of the water dictate the density of the seawater, density is not neglected in the experiment.

PASSAGE IV

17. D The quake in Study 4 was a 6.8 magnitude. You can see by referring to Table 2 that this magnitude is described as ruinous.

18. H Since chimneys collapse in a destructive quake (one of 6.1 to 6.5), and since a disastrous quake (one of 7.1 to 7.3) is stronger than a destructive quake, you could reasonably assume that chimneys would be destroyed in a disastrous quake (among other things that would occur).

19. B As given in Table 2, a fairly strong quake has a magnitude of 4.5 to 4.8. Using Figure 1 and a straightedge (the edge of your answer sheet) to see how many quakes were greater than 4.8, you can determine that there are 7. You could also use Table 1 and simply count the number of quakes greater than 4.8.

20. J If the study on March 2 was conducted in an area of poorly constructed houses, the fact that those houses collapsed might not be a fair indication of the effects of the 6.8 magnitude quake. The second researcher could then point out that had the houses been well built, they would not have collapsed and therefore the effect and description of the 6.8 magnitude quake are inaccurate, biased, and flawed.

21. B From Table 1, you can determine that the effects caused by heavy trucks come from quakes of about 3.7 magnitude. From Table 2, you can see that a 3.7 quake would be described as slight; therefore, the best choice is **B**. Quakes under 3.0 can be detected only by instruments, so you can eliminate choice **A**. The magnitude would have to be 4.5 or greater to wake up those who sleep, so you can eliminate choice **C**. You aren't given any information about cracking of thin walls, so you can eliminate choice **D**.

22. J The quake measured in Study 11 has a magnitude of 7.1. Since an increase of 1 on the Richter scale means 10 times as great, an increase of 2 would mean 100 times as great. On December 1, the quake was 5.0; an increase of about 2 would give 7.1, or approximately 100 times greater.

PASSAGE V

23. D From Table 1, you can see that ethanol and propanol are from the homologous series of alcohols. And information given in the opening paragraph states that the physical properties of these change gradually in the series. Therefore, ethanol and propanol have different physical properties.

24. J Comparing each series in Table 1, you can see that alcohols differ from alkanes and alkenes in that they contain oxygen (O), so they contain atoms other than carbon and hydrogen.

25. A From Table 2, you can see that as the number of carbon atoms increases, the energy of combustion decreases. Choice **A** shows the only graph with the x value increasing and the y value decreasing.

26. G If you analyze the formula column in Table 2, you'll notice that methane CH_4 has 1 carbon atom and 4 hydrogen atoms. As another C is added, making ethane, two more H's are added, giving C_2H_6. In propane, another C is added and two more H's are added, giving C_3H_8. The general formula would be C_nH_{2n+2}, since as you add a C, you double the number of C's and add 2. You could also work this problem by plugging 1, 2, and 3 into the answer choices to see which would give you the formula in the formula column.

27. C If the formula for methane is CH_4 and one atom of Cl swaps with one atom of hydrogen, the outcome of chloromethane would be CH_3Cl, and hydrogen chloride (must have a Cl) would be HCl, so the representation would be $CH_3Cl + HCl$.

PASSAGE VI

28. H From the data, you can see that when resistance increases, the current decreases; therefore, an inverse relationship exists. You may have also noticed mathematically that from the Ohm's law equation, $V = IR$ is in the form of an inverse variation between I and R. To keep V constant, as I increases, R would have to decrease.

29. A If two 12-ohm resistors in series produce the same current as one 24-ohm resistor, then the only logical conclusion is that resistances are additive in series circuits.

30. G By carefully reviewing Figures 3 and 4 and comparing them to the other figures, you can conclude that parallel circuits have all resistors positioned parallel to one another.

31. D From the data given for Figure 1, since R at 0 gives I at 0.50 and R at 1 gives I at 0.48 and so on, you can see that as R increases, I decreases very slowly.

32. G Since electricity follows the path of least resistance, if there is just one path without any resistance, the current would flow from one terminal of the battery to the other, resulting in a short circuit.

33. B From Figure 3, it can be determined that when R is 12, I is 1.5, so the ratio is 12 to 1.5, which can be reduced to 8 : 1 (12 divided by 1.5 equals 8 divided by 1).

PASSAGE VII

34. G The Chemoelectric Theory involves intermittent electrical impulses, so applying intermittent electrical impulses would approximate the activity. Choice **F** mentions a constant low-level voltage, but the voltage should be intermittent.

35. A The Chemoelectric and Chemoaffinity Theories each mention the importance of proper or adequate nutrition.

36. F The Chemoelectric Theory discusses the establishment of neural pathways but doesn't touch upon neuron diversity.

37. D Each of the theories discusses the genetic code or genetics as a basic element.

38. G If the Chemoaffinity Theory is correct, then according to the last sentence of the theory, *the proper level of hormones must also be maintained.*

39. D The frog experiment demonstrates that nerve growth and synaptic contact occur with remarkable precision and selectivity but doesn't demonstrate any of the three theories. There is no reference to electrical stimuli, choice **A,** to chemical identifications, choice **B,** or to vibration frequencies, choice **C.**

40. H Since the Chemoelectric Theory is based on the establishment and growth of neural pathways in response to electrical stimuli, then a study showing this growth without electrical stimuli would most weaken or even contradict the theory.

The ACT Writing Test, which is optional, requires the composition of an essay on a topic familiar to high school students. The prompt presents two sides to an issue, such as requiring school uniforms, allowing junk foods in cafeterias, or mandating physical education classes, and asks students to write an essay that presents their views on the topic. The essay topics are ones that all high school students should be able to write about, and allows them to take one side or the other or to present their own perspective.

The best essays are those that make the most effective use of logical argument and specific supporting detail in language that is clear and correct. A few minor mechanical errors do not injure the essay's score. Examinees have one half-hour to plan and write their essays. The essays are graded by experienced professional readers on a six-point scale.

The scored samples on the ACT website use essays of only one or two paragraphs to illustrate the lowest grades, while the high scoring papers have at least four paragraphs. A very long paper written with no marked paragraph divisions, that is, an essay of several paragraphs in length and content but without the indentations to separate the paragraphs, would receive a good score, but it would receive an even better grade if the paragraph divisions were clear.

Your readers are not, as you may suppose, combing your essay for errors such as split infinitives. They are looking for specific details, for concrete evidence of some kind used to support your points. Perhaps the most obvious difference between the content of the good upper-half essay (scored a 4, 5, or 6) and the content of the weak lower-half paper (a 3, 2, or 1) is the inclusion of supporting detail. Before you begin to write, jot down as many good supporting details as you can think of, and use the best ones in your essay.

The exam provides one and only one topic for your essay. The topic will be familiar enough to allow all the students who take the exam to find something to say in their essays. The topic will not be controversial, and it will not require any specialized information.

Your essay must be completed in 30 minutes.

It does not matter which side you take so long as you complete the tasks set by the question and write well. It is theoretically possible that a top-scoring essay could argue for the extermination of all English composition teachers — although it is unlikely that a prompt that would invite such a response on the exam. Your score is determined by the coherence of your essay and the quality of your writing, not by the political correctness or incorrectness of what you say.

Writing the Essay

There is no single right way to approach writing a timed essay. If you and your teacher are satisfied with the way you handle a 30-minute essay, you can skip this section and continue to write your essays your way. If you are not confident about your technique, consider the following straightforward approach.

STEP ONE. Read the prompt very carefully. Highlight or underline the key words in the assignment. Reread the assignment. Let the nature of the assignment determine the structure of your essay.

STEP TWO. Before you begin to write, take some time to think about what your essay will contain. Decide which side you will take. (Pro? Con? Pro with some reservations? Con with some reservations?)

Next write down any usable specific details that support your position. List as many as you can think of, and decide later which ones you can use.

Determine, if you can, how many paragraphs you will write and what each will be about. Let the question and your evidence help you to determine how you will put your essay together.

STEP THREE. Carefully write your essay. Keep in mind what the tasks are, what each paragraph is to contain, and what specific details you use. Take some extra time with the transitions from one paragraph to another.

STEP FOUR. Reread your essay, looking carefully for errors in the spelling, punctuation, and the grammar. Make sure the writing is legible.

As a final check, ask yourself these questions:

- Does the essay focus on the topic and complete the assigned task?
- Is the essay coherently developed and consistent in argument?
- Does the essay use specific supporting detail?
- Is the writing grammatically and structurally correct?

If you can answer "yes" to these questions, you can go on with confidence.

Nine Suggestions for Essay Writing

1. Try to be genuinely interested in the topic.

2. Don't worry about the answer you think "they" want you to write.

3. Don't simply repeat the language of the prompt.

4. Don't be afraid to be honest.

5. Avoid clichés.

6. Write naturally.

7. Choose your words with some thought and don't use words if you're unsure of their meaning.

8. Don't be afraid to use contractions, figures of speech, even slang, but do so tactfully.

9. Don't be wish-washy.

Sample Student Essays and Analysis

The following pages present student essays written under Writing
Test conditions. The papers are reproduced exactly as they were written, so they contain some mechanical errors and some bad writing.
The high school students wrote the essays in 30 minutes or less, the
time limit on the Writing Test. The scoring guide used to grade the
essays is given first, followed by sample prompts, student essays, and
a brief comment on each.

Scoring Guide. Since the student has only 30 minutes to write the
essay, minor errors of grammar or mechanics will not affect the score.
The essays scored at 6 will not be errorless — they are, after all, first
drafts — but they will be superior to the other essays.

SCORE of 6

These consistently competent essays are characterized by the following:

- the coherent expression of a perspective (or perspectives) on
  the topic
- good organization and development, with relevant supporting
  details
- command of standard written English with a range of vocabulary and variety of syntax

SCORE of 5

These competent essays are characterized by the following:

- the coherent expression of a perspective (or perspectives) on
  the topic
- generally good organization and development, with some supporting details
- good handling of standard written English with some range of
  vocabulary and variety of syntax

SCORE of 4

These adequately competent essays are characterized by the following:

- the expression of a perspective (or perspectives) on the topic
- adequate organization and development with some supporting details
- adequate handling of standard written English, but with minimal variety of syntax and some grammatical or diction errors

SCORE of 3

These marginal papers are characterized by the following:

- failure to cover fully the required task
- weak organization and/or development
- failure to use relevant supporting detail
- several errors of grammar, diction, and syntax

SCORE of 2

These inadequate papers are characterized by the following:

- failure to cover the assignment
- poor organization and development
- lack of supporting detail
- many errors of grammar, diction, and syntax

SCORE of 1

These incompetent papers are characterized by the following:

- failure to cover the assignment
- very poor organization and development
- errors of grammar, syntax, and diction so frequent as to interfere with meaning
- extreme brevity

ACT Essay

Sample Prompt. Many school boards across the country have banned the selling of high calorie soft drinks and snacks such as potato chips and candy bars in cafeterias and vending machines on high school campuses. They argue that the easy availability of junk foods encourages poor eating habits that lead to obesity and other health problems. Opponents of the ban contend that the removal of these foods does nothing to change students' eating habits and infringes upon their right to choose. In your opinion, should high calorie–low food value soft drinks and snacks be banned from sale on high school campuses?

In your essay, take a position on this question. You may write about either of the two sides given here, or you may present a different point of view. Use specific examples and reasons to support your position.

You have 30 minutes to plan and write your essay.

Sample Essay #1 — Lower-Level Score

I agree that junk food and high calorie snacks such as candy bars and potato chips should not be sold in vending machines or in school cafeterias. These drinks and snacks encourage bad eating habits. They can lead to health problems like being overweight. It stands to reason that if these foods and drinks are not available in schools, high school students will not buy them and impair their health and become obese.

It will also save money that could have been spent on books or on foods with greater health benefits like fresh fruits. If vending machines sold fresh fruits in season such as apples and pears in fall and winter and peaches and plums in spring and summer, student's health problems would not only improve, but they would not be overweight and would look and feel better. These are good reasons for not selling junk food in high schools.

Evaluating the Essay

This essay makes the writer's position clear, but fails to support this position effectively.

In the first paragraph, the first two sentences depend almost entirely on repeating the diction of the prompt. The third sentence simply repeats the ideas of the first two.

The paragraph does at least make one point, though it is a simple one, and does use some detail (apples, pears, etc.). Like the first, the paragraph is repetitive and bland.

The mechanics of the essay are weak, with errors of parallelism, diction, vague pronoun reference, agreement, and punctuation.

If the essay were better, its extreme brevity might not count so heavily against it.

Sample Essay #2 — Upper-Level Score

I have mixed views about the ban of junk foods and drinks which has been in effect at my school (Walt Whitman High) for several years. The profits from the vending machines which used to sell Coke and Pepsi went to the students activities fund. When they changed to orange juice and Snapple, the profits went way down. The cost of some sports events and other student activities like the prom and the senior play were higher. This loss of revenue is one disadvantage of the change, though the principal claims the profits from the machines improve each year.

To my unscientific eye, the health and habits of my classmates are pretty much the same. Although they can't buy junk food on campus, they still can get them at stores and machines near the school. There is no visible sign that the number of kids who are overweight has decreased.

The one success of the healthier food and drink campaign is bottled water. Bottled water (though it is way overpriced for just water) outsells the fruit juices in the machines. Why haven't the fruit juices caught on? Advertisements. TV is filled with ads showing gorgeous high school girls at parties drinking Coke or Dr. Pepper. Other ads show buff guys playing volleyball at the beach and drinking bottled waters. But there is never an oj or an apple juice in sight.

I can understand the reasons behind the ban of junk foods on campus, but I don't believe it has had much effect on what high school

students eat and drink. Despite the minor success of bottled water sales, students still prefer Pepsi to cranberry juice and potato chips to raw carrots, and are willing to drive or even walk to the stores that sell what they like.

Evaluating the Essay

This essay is confident and well written. Though the writer refuses to support only one side of the argument, the essay makes its position clear. Each of the four paragraphs is coherent, and the arguments are convincingly backed with specific details. The sentences are varied, and the vocabulary is relaxed and mature. At all times the prose is straightforward, free of clichés, and clear.

Sample Essay #3 — Lower-Level Score

School boards who decide to ban junk food and high calorie sodas from high-school vending machines are attempting to do a good thing, protect students from bad nutrition and its affects. Unfortunately in doing this, they are overstepping boundaries. We should all have the right to choose what we eat.

The decision to ban certain foods is part of a "Big Brother" attitude in which authorities more and more want to eliminate individual choice and restrict the students right to choose. It makes sense for school boards to have strict rules about weapons on campus - or drugs and alcohol - because in addition to the legal issues, these present a threat not only to those who use them but also other students.

Foods that aren't good for us are not illegal. Restricting them should be left up to parents and students. It is a good idea to provide students with information about the dangers of some foods, but that is a far cry from banning such foods and drinks from high school vending machines.

Evaluating the Essay

This essay is better than Sample Essay #1, but still a lower-half performance. It has only one point to make so the essay does not develop;

it simply repeats itself. It makes little use of supporting detail, and there are two or three mechanical or grammatical errors in each of the three undeveloped paragraphs.

Answers to Your Questions about the ACT Writing Test

Should I make an outline before I write my essay?

If you can write better essays without an outline, don't change your writing habits. Your reader will be looking for good organization and development in your essay; an outline (or some sort of pre-writing), however brief, will probably help you to organize your ideas. The outline itself (or any notes you make) will not be graded or counted in the scoring.

Should I write a five-paragraph essay?

If you write a well-organized, well-developed, specific, and interesting essay, no one will notice how many paragraphs it contains. If you are most comfortable with the five-paragraph format, continue to use it. Otherwise, be sure that you write in paragraphs and that you write more than one. The lowest scored student sample essays have only one paragraph; the essays with the highest scores have four or more. Rather than deciding in advance how many paragraphs you will write, let the logic of your essay determine the number.

How long an essay should I write?

You will not be graded on the length of your essay, and you have only 30 minutes. Keep in mind that very short essays will probably not be sufficiently developed. Each essay is scored by two readers using a scale from 1 to 6. In the sample essays, the highest scores are essays of four to six paragraphs and about 400 words in length. In the lower-half of the scale, the range is from two-paragraph essays of 185 words, to those at the bottom with one paragraph and 100 words.

This is not to say that the longer your essay is, the higher your score. Padding out your paper with repetition or verbose phrasing will lower your score. Before you begin to write, plan your essay to cover the topic fully with specific supporting detail.

Are spelling and punctuation important?

The readers pay no attention to one or two minor spelling or punctuation errors. They understand that your essay is a first draft written in only 30 minutes. But if the mechanical errors in a paper are so numerous that they interfere with your communicating meaning, those errors will count heavily against you.

How important is correct grammar?

Even the best papers (two scores of 6) may have occasional errors. In papers in the lower-half of the grading scale, errors of grammar are common.

How important is good handwriting?

Readers make an effort to avoid being influenced by good or bad handwriting, but there may be an unconscious hostility to a paper that is very hard to read. Make your writing as legible as you can.

Is there a reward for creativity in an essay?

It depends on what you mean by creativity. If you mean writing a poem or a letter or a dialogue or a diary when the question calls for an essay, the answer is an emphatic "No." If you mean writing an essay that is on the topic and has an individual voice, original ideas, wit, and style, the answer is "Yes, indeed."

How important is the use of detail or specific examples?

It is crucial. The question will almost certainly ask you to give an example or specific details to support your argument. One of the most obvious differences between papers in the upper- and the lower-half of the scoring scale is their use, or failure to use, specific examples.

What if I don't finish my essay?

The readers are told again and again to reward students for what they do well. If you have left out only a few sentences of conclusion to your essay, it may well not affect your score at all. If you have written three quarters of your essay on the topic, you will certainly get full credit for all you have written, and it may be close to a complete answer. Do not get depressed if you haven't finished and let your disappointment harm your performance in other sections of the test; perhaps you did not finish because what you were writing was so good.

Do you have you any suggestions about style?

1. Write naturally.

2. Avoid clichés. If the topic suggests a familiar proverb or quotation to you, resist the temptation to quote. Fifty thousand other papers will have used it already.

How many readers will grade my essay?

Two readers grade each essay on a scale from 1 to 6. If there is more than a two-point discrepancy between the two grades, a third reader will score the essay. None of the readers is aware of the scores the other reader or readers have given a paper.

Is there any specific course required before I take the Writing Test?

No. Almost all students who take the exam have had one to three high school English classes, but most have not a had a course exclusively concerned with writing.

What scores will I receive?

The scores reported to you and to the colleges you designate will include a scaled score, from 1 to 36, that reflects the performance on the Writing Test and the English Test combined. A second Writing Test subscore on a 2 to 12 scale that reflects your scores on the Writing Test will also be reported.

How should I practice writing essays before the exam?

Take your practice exams seriously and pay close attention to the time so that you become accustomed to finishing your essay in the 30 minutes allowed. Be sure to write more than one paragraph.Ask a friend (or better yet, two friends) or any one or two people able to judge writing to read and score your essay using the scoring guide on pages 302-303 of this book.

You can also use the student essays printed here to refine your editorial, or revising, skills. The essays in the lower-half of the scale are especially likely to contain a number of mechanical errors or weaknesses of style that aren't specified in the comments on them. If you can find and correct these errors, you will be able to avoid similar mistakes in your own writing.

Sample Prompts for Practice

Sample 1

The state legislature is debating whether or not to make physical education a required subject in all three years of high school throughout the state. If physical education classes were optional, many students who lack the natural athletic ability of their peers would be spared acute embarrassment. And in some school grades in physical education classes distort the academic grade point averages. On the other hand, American teenagers do not get nearly enough exercise to maintain good health.

Write an essay in which you support or oppose physical education classes in high school. Or, if you prefer, take an alternate position. Use specific reasons and details to support your argument.

Sample 2

The school board is debating whether or not to allow a series of commercially produced television programs on varied academic subjects to be shown in high school classrooms. The programs are geared for a high school audience, and have been universally praised by both students and teachers. However, all of the programs include at least five minutes of advertisement in each 30-minute segment. Do you think films that include commercial messages should be shown in high school classes?

Write an essay that states your point of view on this issue. Support your argument with reasons and examples.

CLIFFS QUICK REVIEW